how to IMPROVE YOUR BRIDGE

The Fourth Book of Bridge

BY ALFRED SHEINWOLD

Published by
Melvin Powers
WILSHIRE BOOK COMPANY
12015 Sherman Road
No. Hollywood, California 91605
Telephone: (213) 875-1711

© 1963 "How to Improve Your Bridge"
and © 1956 "Fourth Book of Bridge"
by Sterling Publishing Co., Inc.
419 Fourth Ave., New York 16, N.Y.

Manufactured in the United States of America
Library of Congress Catalogue Card No.: 63–14297

Printed by
HAL LEIGHTON PRINTING COMPANY
P.O. Box 3952
North Hollywood, California 91605
Telephone: (213) 983-1105

ISBN 0-87980-059-3

Table of Contents

FOREWORD

This book is meant for you if you have already played a fair amount of bridge and if you want to improve your game—particularly your bidding.

The 4-3-2-1 Point Count is used throughout, but the purpose of the book is to lift you past the adding-machine stage up to the rarefied heights of expert judgment. More than 600 illustrative hands are used for this purpose, with the quizzes reinforcing the lessons of the main text.

The bidding advice in this book applies to rubber bridge, but most of it can be used profitably in duplicate tournaments. The "system" recommended is the method followed by the majority of the leading American players.

Your attention is called particularly to the discussion of forcing and non-forcing bids in the various chapters. In most cases all of the experts agree, and you will be well advised to go along with them; in a few cases, they disagree, and here you may use your own judgment—provided that you make sure that your various partners always know what your bids mean.

It isn't necessary to read the entire book at one sitting. Take it a few pages, or a chapter, at a time. Refer to it from time to time, especially after a losing session; it may help you get your revenge the next time.

1. Opening Bids of One in a Suit

THE "STANDARD" REQUIREMENTS

What does your partner expect when you open the bidding with one in a suit?

He expects you to have some sort of biddable suit, with a count of 14 points or more. If you actually have an unbiddable suit or fewer than 14 points, you should have a convincing reason for your bid.

What does your partner expect when you *fail* to open the bidding?

He expects you to have a hand that isn't worth an opening bid. If you fail to open with a biddable hand you should have either a convincing reason or an appointment with a reliable oculist.

These simple rules are enough for family bridge. Slavishly followed outside of the family, these rules will give you the basis of a good losing game! If you insist on winning, however, you will need something more than beginners' tactics.

WHEN TO ALTER THE COUNT

A point is not always a point. There's nothing holy about the 4-3-2-1 count. Various bridge authorities have suggested other counts (such as 3-2-1 or 7-5-3-2-1, etc.), but the fact is that no count is completely accurate.

Don't let this fact upset you. Just make a mental note of

what is wrong with the count and be guided by these consider-ations in borderline situations.

The ace is really worth more than 4 points. The queen is worth less than 2 points. The jack is worth less than 1 point. A king is a king, however (3 points).

In most hands the difference isn't worth thinking about. The strength of one card is balanced by the weakness of another, so that the 4-3-2-1 point count gives a very good picture of the true value of the hand. The difference is worth thinking about when all the trifles go in the same direction.

1. ♠ A 6 3 2   ♥ A 5 3   ♦ A 4 3   ♣ 5 4 2

This hand is worth more than a mere 12 points. If it con-tained a couple of queens or jacks, the pluses would be balanced by minuses. In this case there are only pluses.

2. ♠ Q J 6 3   ♥ Q J 5   ♦ Q J 4   ♣ Q J 5

This hand is not worth a full 12 points. In this case there are only minuses. Mind you, this hand will be very valuable if your partner has a sprinkling of kings and aces, but its independent value is far less than that of the previous three-ace hand.

Aces and Kings: There are eight aces and kings in the deck, and the opening bidder should have two or more of them. There is no such thing as an opening bid of one in a suit with neither an ace nor a king in the hand.

3. ♠ Q J 10 9   ♥ Q J 10   ♦ Q J 10   ♣ Q J 10

This hand is all right for support or for defense, but it is not worth an opening bid.

4. ♠ Q J 10 9 8   ♥ Q J 10 9 8   ♦ Q J   ♣ Q

This seems to be a 14-point hand (11 points for high cards and 3 points for distribution), but never bother to add up the points in such a hand for the purpose of *opening* the bidding. Just remember that an aceless and kingless hand is not an open-ing bid no matter where you sit nor what the score is.

5. ♠ Q J 2   ♥ Q J 10 9 4   ♦ A Q   ♣ Q J 3

Bid one heart. It is just barely possible to have a sensible opening bid with only one card above the queen.

Combination Values: The value of a picture card is increased when it is accompanied by a higher card in the same suit. For example, the ace-king of the same suit are worth more than an ace and king in different suits. Most experts will open the bidding with:

6. ♠ A K 10 6 3   ♥ 8 7 3   ♦ 4 2   ♣ A 4 2

They will not open the hand if it is changed to:

7. ♠ A 10 6 3 2   ♥ 8 7 3   ♦ K 4   ♣ A 4 2

The principle applies particularly to queens and jacks. Thus, Q-J-x is worth more than Q-x-x in one suit and J-x-x in another. A-Q-x is worth more than A-x-x and Q-x-x. Give full value to the queen or jack in such combinations as A-J-x, K-Q-x, or K-J-x. It isn't necessary to tell an experienced player to do likewise with such combinations as A-K-Q-J, A-K-Q, A-K-J, A-Q-J, and K-Q-J.

8. ♠ 8 7 3   ♥ A Q J 7 5   ♦ A 8 5   ♣ 9 3

This is a borderline opening bid of one heart. Nobody can quarrel much with a bid or with a pass.

9. ♠ Q 7 3   ♥ A 9 7 5 3   ♦ A 8 5   ♣ J 3

No expert would open this hand, except possibly as a shaded third-hand bid. The hand has been greatly weakened by scattering the queen and jack instead of combining them.

Unguarded Picture Cards: Every experienced player knows that a singleton king is often worth far less than a guarded king. It's worth more than a singleton deuce, of course, but it certainly isn't worth a full 3 points. Much the same is true of singleton queens or jacks, and even of doubleton queens or jacks.

Deduct 1 point from the normal value of any singleton picture card or from any doubleton picture card except the combinations A-K, A-Q, and K-x.

$K = 2$ Q or Q-x $= 1$ J or J-x $= 0$ K-Q $= 4$
          K-J $= 3$ Q-J $= 2$ A-J $= 4$

To these high-card values you will, of course, add the normal 2 points for the singleton and one for the doubleton.

MINIMUM AND BORDERLINE BIDS

Most experts believe in opening light at rubber bridge. Some avoid a light opening bid in duplicate bridge. Either style is playable, provided that the partnership is aware of which style is being used. In this book we'll assume that the partnership favors the light opening bid.

Where do you draw the line? Up to a certain point, an opening bid, though light, is sensible. Beyond that point, the opening bid is too light and not sensible.

Practically every experienced player knows when he has a doubtful opening bid. When you have such a hand, you can decide for or against the bid by asking yourself these questions:

Is this hand really worth its point count?

Will I have a convenient rebid if my partner responds in a new suit?

Will my bid indicate a favorable opening lead if we become the defenders?

CHOICE OF SUIT

As a beginner you were probably taught to choose between biddable suits on this basis: Begin with the longer of two suits that are unequal in length; begin with the higher of two suits that are equally long.

An experienced player departs from this rule much more than he follows it. Modern expert practice follows these lines:

6-5: If the hand is strong, bid the 6-card suit first. Otherwise, act as though both suits were 5-carders.

5-5: If the suits are touching, bid the higher suit first. If the suits are spades and clubs, begin with clubs unless the club suit is quite weak. If the suits are spades-diamonds or hearts-clubs, bid the major suit first unless the major suit is so weak that you're reluctant to treat it as a rebiddable suit.

5-4: With a strong hand (about 19 points or more), bid the longer suit first. With hands of lesser strength, bid the higher suit when they are touching (spades-hearts, hearts-diamonds, or diamonds-clubs). When the suits don't touch, bid the longer suit first, except that it is permissible to treat a weak 5-card suit as though it were a 4-carder (in which case you follow the rule for 4-4 suits).

4-4: With touching suits, bid the higher suit first. In other cases, bid the minor suit first. (Occasionally, you may get a better result by bidding the major suit first—especially when a response in your doubleton will allow you to bid two of your minor suit or two notrump.)

4-4-4-1: Bid the suit below the singleton (bid spades if the singleton is a club). If one of the suits is very weak, disregard it and treat the hand as a 4-4 two-suiter.

6-4: Bid the 6-card suit first. Bid the 4-card suit next if you can do so at the level of one. Otherwise, rebid the 6-carder before showing the 4-card suit.

OPENING IN THIRD OR FOURTH POSITION

If your partner favors light opening bids, there's no need to open on garbage in third or fourth position. Since your partner has passed, he will seldom have more than 9 or 10 points in high cards; and the hand is not likely to "belong" to your side unless you have a normal sound opening bid.

There are 40 points in the deck, and the hand doesn't belong clearly to either side when the points are split 20-20 or 21-19. You need about 12 points in high cards, after partner has passed, to feel reasonably hopeful that the combined count is as high as 22 points.

You therefore tend to open in third or fourth position with 12 points or more in high cards. You needn't worry about your rebid, since you can afford to pass even if your partner responds in a new suit.

You may even open in third position with only 10 points in high cards when you can bid a suit that will suggest a favorable opening lead.

10. ♠ 8 6 3   ♡ K Q J 9 4   ◇ 7 4   ♣ A 9 2

Bid one heart in third position, but pass in fourth position. The idea is to suggest a heart opening lead if your left-hand opponent becomes declarer. You intend to pass your partner's response.

11. ♠ K 6 3   ♡ K J 9 4 2   ◇ 7 4   ♣ K 9 2

Pass in any position. You have no reason to suppose that a heart opening lead will be better than any other. You don't bid in third position on *any* 10-point hand, but only when the advantage of suggesting a favorable lead outweighs the risk of bidding on a bad hand.

A borderline fourth-hand bid should be passed if it is weak in both majors. Tend to bid such a hand if you have strength in both majors, particularly if you have a biddable spade suit. The player who holds spades enjoys an advantage in competitive auctions, since the opponents may be reluctant to overcall at the level of two and can be outbid cheaply even if they do come in.

12. ♠ A J 8 7 4   ♡ K 9 6 2   ◇ A 5   ♣ 8 3

Bid one spade in third or fourth position. This borderline hand has strength in both majors.

13. ♠ A 5   ♡ 8 3   ◇ A J 8 7 4   ♣ K 9 6 2

Pass in fourth position. It is too risky to open a borderline hand that is weak in both majors. In third position, you may either pass or bid one diamond.

QUIZ No. 1

You are the dealer, with each of the following hands. What do you say? (Answers to quizzes begin on page 148.)

14. ♠ K Q J 9 7 6   ♡ Q J 4   ◇ Q 10 8   ♣ 7
15. ♠ A Q J 9 7 6   ♡ Q J 4   ◇ Q 10 8   ♣ 7
16. ♠ A Q J 9 7 6   ♡ K J 4   ◇ Q J 8   ♣ 7
17. ♠ A 9 7 6 4   ♡ K J   ◇ Q J 8   ♣ Q J 7
18. ♠ K 9 7 6 4   ♡ K J   ◇ Q J 8   ♣ Q J 7
19. ♠ A 9 7 6 4   ♡ A 4   ◇ Q J 8   ♣ Q J 7
20. ♠ A 9 7 6 4   ♡ 8 4   ◇ 2   ♣ A K J 7 3
21. ♠ A K J 7 3   ♡ 8 4   ◇ 2   ♣ A 9 7 6 4
22. ♠ A K J 7 3   ♡ A 5   ◇ 2   ♣ J 9 7 6 4
23. ♠ J 9 7 6 4   ♡ A 5   ◇ 2   ♣ A K J 7 3
24. ♠ J 9 7 6 4   ♡ A 5   ◇ 8 2   ♣ A K J 7
25. ♠ J 9 7 6 4   ♡ A Q J 9 3   ◇ A 2   ♣ 5
26. ♠ K J 7 6 4   ♡ A 2   ◇ A Q J 9 3   ♣ 5
27. ♠ J 9 7 6 4   ♡ A 2   ◇ A K J 9 3   ♣ 5
28. ♠ 9 7 6 4 2   ♡ A 2   ◇ A K Q J 3   ♣ 5
29. ♠ A J 9 3 2   ♡ K 10 9 6 4   ◇ A Q   ♣ 4
30. ♠ A J 9 3 2   ♡ K 10 9 6   ◇ A Q 3   ♣ 4
31. ♠ A J 9 3   ♡ K 10 9 6 4   ◇ A Q 3   ♣ 4
32. ♠ A Q J 9   ♡ K Q 10 6 4   ◇ A Q 3   ♣ 4
33. ♠ K J 8 5   ♡ 7 3   ◇ A Q 10 9 6   ♣ A 8
34. ♠ K J 8 5   ♡ 7 3   ◇ A 8   ♣ A Q 10 9 6
35. ♠ 7 3   ♡ K J 8 5   ◇ A 8   ♣ A Q 10 9 6
36. ♠ 7 3   ♡ A 8   ◇ K J 8 5   ♣ A Q 10 9 6
37. ♠ A Q 9 5   ♡ K J 6   ◇ 7 2   ♣ K J 10 4
38. ♠ A Q 9 5   ♡ K J 6   ◇ 7 3 2   ♣ K J 10
39. ♠ A K 9 5   ♡ 9 8 6 2   ◇ 3 2   ♣ A Q 10
40. ♠ J 8 5 3   ♡ K J 7 3   ◇ A 6 2   ♣ A Q
41. ♠ J 8 5 3   ♡ A 6 2   ◇ K J 7 3   ♣ A Q
42. ♠ J 8 5 3   ♡ A Q   ◇ A 6 2   ♣ K J 7 3
43. ♠ K J 7 3   ♡ A Q   ◇ A 6 2   ♣ J 8 5 3

44. ♠ A Q J 3   ♡ A Q 4   ◇ 7 2   ♣ K Q J 3
45. ♠ A Q J 3   ♡ A Q 7 4   ◇ 7   ♣ K Q J 3
46. ♠ K J 8 3   ♡ 9   ◇ K Q 9 6   ♣ A J 3 2
47. ♠ 6   ♡ Q 10 7 2   ◇ K J 8 5   ♣ A K Q 2
48. ♠ Q 8 7 3   ♡ K Q 6 2   ◇ A Q J 4   ♣ 2
49. ♠ J 8 7 3   ♡ A Q 6 2   ◇ A K J 4   ♣ 2

QUIZ No. 2

You are third hand after two passes, with each of the following hands. What do you say?

50. ♠ 9 8 7 6 2   ♡ A K 9   ◇ K 7 5   ♣ 8 2
51. ♠ A K 7 6 2   ♡ 9 8 3   ◇ K 7 5   ♣ 8 2
52. ♠ K Q J 9 8 3   ♡ 9 8   ◇ 8 7 5   ♣ 6 2
53. ♠ K Q J 9 8 4   ♡ 9 8   ◇ K Q 5   ♣ 6 2
54. ♠ Q J 7 6 4   ♡ 9 8 3   ◇ A K 5   ♣ 6 2
55. ♠ Q J 7 6 4   ♡ Q 8 3   ◇ A K 5   ♣ 6 2
56. ♠ J 7 6 4 2   ♡ A J 3   ◇ A K 5   ♣ 6 2
57. ♠ A K 9 5   ♡ 7 6 3   ◇ 8 7 5   ♣ K Q 5
58. ♠ A K J 5   ♡ 7 6 3 2   ◇ 8 5   ♣ A K 5
59. ♠ A K J 5   ♡ K J 3   ◇ 8 5   ♣ A J 9 4
60. ♠ Q J 9 4   ♡ A Q J 8 5   ◇ K 5 2   ♣ 7
61. ♠ K J 9 4   ♡ A K J 8 5   ◇ K 5 2   ♣ 7

QUIZ No. 3

You are fourth hand, after three passes, with each of the following hands. What do you say?

62. ♠ Q 7 3 2   ♡ A K J 6   ◇ 9 7 4   ♣ 8 5
63. ♠ Q 7 3 2   ♡ A K J 6   ◇ Q 7 4   ♣ 8 5
64. ♠ Q J 7 2   ♡ A K J 6   ◇ 9 7 4   ♣ 8 5
65. ♠ A Q 9 6 4   ♡ K 6 2   ◇ K 7 4   ♣ 8 5
66. ♠ 8 5   ♡ K 6 2   ◇ K 7 4   ♣ A Q 9 6 4
67. ♠ 8 5   ♡ K 6 2   ◇ K Q 4   ♣ A Q J 6 4
68. ♠ A K 8 4   ♡ J 9 4 2   ◇ 7 4   ♣ K Q 10

2. Responding to One of a Suit

THE "STANDARD" REQUIREMENTS

Most bridge books tell you how to count your distributional points as well as your high-card points for responses. One trouble with this scheme is that you never know whether or not to count points for shortness in partner's bid suit. Another disadvantage is that the total possible count exceeds 40 points when you count for length and for shortness, and that you cannot then rely on 33 points to produce a slam.

The idea of converting all kinds of strength to one kind of points is a good one when you have to tell beginners what to do. Advanced players don't need this kind of guidance; and, in fact, they don't follow it.

Most good players classify a hand mentally as "10 points with a singleton," or "a good 12 points with a doubleton," or some such rating, depending on the nature of the hand. They know the value of singletons and doubletons, and they make allowance for this value in choosing a bid. At the same time, they always know the *accurate* high-card count of the hand.

Before we begin to discuss the refinements of expert responding, let's review the standard requirements, as most players know them:

Notrump Responses: 1 NT, 6-10 points; 2 NT, 13-15 points, 3 NT, 16 or 17 points.

Raises: Single, 6-10 points; double, 13-17 points; triple, distributional.

New Suits: 1-over-1, 6 to 17 points; 2-over-1 (non-jump), 10-17 points; jump takeout, 18 or more points.

HOW MANY RESPONSES?

When your partner, the opening bidder, has a good hand, he will give you more than one chance to respond. When he has close to a minimum opening bid, he will depend on *you* to judge the combined strength.

To put it in a general way, you will drop the bidding like a hot potato when you have a bad hand; you will push on aggressively when you have a good hand; and you will make a tentative bid with a middling hand.

This rough scheduling makes it more specific:

6 to 9 points: Respond once but then get out as cheaply as possible unless partner shows unmistakable strength.

10 to 12 points: Plan to respond twice, even if partner shows a near-minimum opening bid. You intend to *suggest* a game, not to *invite* one, and certainly not to *demand* one.

13 to 17 points: Keep bidding until game is reached, except in case of an extreme misfit.

18 points or more: Try for a slam.

THE SINGLE RAISE

Most raises are clear-cut. You have fine support for partner's suit and nothing else worth mentioning.

Other raises are far from clear. Your trump support may be doubtful, you may have another suit to bid, or the value of the hand may fall squarely between a single raise and a double raise.

Let's begin our list of close choices with the distinction between major and minor suits. You are happy to raise a major suit; you raise a minor only when you can't think of anything else to do.

For example, partner opens with one heart, and you hold:

69. ♠ K 9 7 2   ♡ A 10 6 4   ◇ 7 3   ♣ 8 7 5

You are delighted to raise to two hearts. You don't give a thought to mentioning the spades. *When a hand is worth only one response, your first duty is to raise a major suit.*

Now assume that your partner opens with one diamond, and that your hand is slightly changed:

70.   ♠ K 9 7 2   ♡ 7 3   ◇ A 10 6 4   ♣ 8 7 5

You bid one spade instead of raising the diamonds.

The same principle applies to double raises. Partner opens with one heart, and you hold:

71.   ♠ K 9 7 2   ♡ A 10 6 4   ◇ 7 3   ♣ A Q 5

You raise to three hearts. The spades are only a small part of the whole picture.

But in response to a diamond bid, you hold:

72.   ♠ K 9 7 2   ♡ 7 3   ◇ A 10 6 4   ♣ A Q 5

You bid one spade rather than three diamonds. You have in mind the advantage of finding a fit in the major suit, but there is the additional problem of avoiding what may be a bad contract of three notrump.

The trouble with the double raise in a minor suit is that partner's rebid is almost invariably three notrump. Often he makes this contract, but sometimes both partners are short and weak in the same suit. Then three notrump goes down, where five of a minor would make.

You can't always avoid this fate, but you have a chance if you show your biddable major before showing the full support for partner's minor suit. This is not a sure-fire solution, since your later raise may seem invitational rather than forcing.

The best solution to the problem of raises in a minor suit was suggested recently by Edgar Kaplan, famous New York expert. His method is to make the *single* raise forcing, and the double raise pre-emptive (weak): the opposite of the normal procedure.

This strong single raise gives you the bidding room you need to find out whether or not you can stop all of the unbid suits. If you can, you confidently bid game in notrump; otherwise, you stay in your minor suit. The weak double raise has enough trump support to be safe, and it has the advantage of making matters difficult for the opponents.

The Kaplan method is recommended for steady partnerships, but it is dangerous in the ordinary pivot game with comparatively strange partners. You can't afford to have a stranger drop your forcing bid (single raise) or wax enthusiastic over your weak bid (double raise).

Sometimes your choice is between a raise and a response of one notrump. Since the raise is more encouraging, prefer the raise with 8 points or more; prefer the notrump response with only 6 or 7 points.

In each of the following cases, assume that partner has opened the bidding with one spade:

73. ♠ Q 7 6   ♡ 9 5 3 2   ◇ K 8 3   ♣ J 5 4

Bid one notrump. With only 6 points, prefer the response of 1 NT.

74. ♠ Q 7 6   ♡ 9 5 3 2   ◇ K 8 3   ♣ K 5 4

Bid two spades. With 8 points, prefer the raise.

75. ♠ Q 7 6 2   ♡ 9 5 3 2   ◇ K 8 3   ♣ J 4

Bid two spades. Only 6 points, but the side doubleton and the four trumps are arguments for the raise.

76. ♠ 9 5 3 2   ♡ Q 7 6   ◇ K 8 3   ♣ J 5 4

Bid one notrump. Despite the four trumps, the distribution is flat. With only 6 points you prefer the notrump response.

We have already discussed the choice between the single raise and the new suit at the level of one (Hands 69 and 70). The same principles apply when you are considering a bid in a new suit at the level of *two*.

Assume that your partner has opened with one spade, and that you hold:

77. ♠ K 7 6   ♡ 10 9 4   ◇ 8 5   ♣ K Q 9 7 3

Bid two spades. The hand isn't worth two bids, so you cannot afford to show the clubs first and the spade support later.

Incidentally, what would you bid if partner opened the bidding with one *heart?*

The hand is a borderline case. You tend towards a raise since you have 8 points in high cards and a side doubleton. You tend away from the raise with three small trumps. Which tendency is stronger?

The more skillful your partner, the more you should tend towards the raise. The raise is more encouraging, better expresses the value of your hand, and is more likely to lead to a good result. If your partner is a poor player, prefer the notrump response. Some of the worst disasters in bridge history have come from the combination of a doubtful player with a doubtful trump suit!

Strengthen the hand a bit:

78. ♠ K 7 6   ♡ 10 9 4   ◇ 8 5   ♣ A K 9 7 3

Now you can afford to respond two clubs whether partner's opening bid has been one spade or one heart. Your hand is worth two bids, and you can afford to show the clubs first and the support for the major suit later.

The result is similar if the additional strength takes the form of better distribution:

79. ♠ K 7 6   ♡ 10 9 4 2   ◇ 5   ♣ K Q 9 7 3

In response to one spade or one heart, your hand is just barely worth two bids. You can show the clubs first and the support for the major suit next. This is a borderline case. There would be no question about it if either black king were changed to an ace.

THE RAISE TO TWO-AND-A-HALF

In the last two examples we have already ventured past the single raise and into the limits of the raise to two-and-a-half. The standard method of showing a hand that is worth more than a single raise but less than a double raise is to bid a new suit first and then show support for the original suit.

The most familiar auction of this kind is:

South	North
1 ♡	2 ♣
2 ♡	3 ♡

Many players forget that the same message is conveyed by:

South	North
1 ♡	2 ♣
2 ◊	2 ♡

Most good players will avoid showing a mere preference for hearts with a doubleton heart. Hence North almost invariably has at least three-card support for hearts for this sequence of bids. North has already shown strength by responding in a new suit at the level of two; he does not have to repeat that he has a good hand by jumping to *three* hearts.

Mind you, there *is* such a bid as *three* hearts in this situation. The point to remember is that North shows one kind of hand for a bid of two hearts, and a better hand for a bid of three hearts.

80. ♠ 9 3   ♡ 10 7 4   ◊ K 9 8   ♣ A K J 6 2

When partner bids one heart, you can afford two responses. You show the clubs, expecting to raise the hearts next. When partner bids diamonds at his second turn, you bid only *two* hearts. You have already shown the value of your hand by bidding two clubs; there is no need for another strong bid.

81. ♠ 9 3   ♡ K 9 8   ◊ K 9 8   ♣ A K J 6 2

With this hand you bid two clubs in response to one heart. When partner then makes a rebid of two diamonds, you jump to *three hearts*. The first response did not show the full value of the hand, and a further strong bid is necessary.

This sort of jump preference usually shows strong *three*-card trump support. If your hand contained *four* trumps, the chances are that you would have begun with a double raise instead of showing your own suit.

In general, the *temporizing* bid in a new suit followed by support of the original suit is used when you have strong trump support but a mediocre hand, or when you have a strong hand but only mediocre trump support. When you are strong in both departments, you can afford a double raise.

THE DOUBLE RAISE

The double raise in a major suit shows strong trump support of four cards or more with a total count of about 13 to 17 points. Unless made by a "passed hand," the double raise in a major is forcing to game.

South	North
1 ♠	?

82. ♠ K J 5 2   ♡ 4 2   ◇ A J 9 3 2   ♣ K 3

Bid three spades. You have strong trump support, together with a count of 12 points in high cards, plus the value of the long diamond suit and the two doubletons.

The double raise is highly satisfactory on this sort of hand for several other reasons, all important. To begin with, the hand has a reasonable quota of aces and kings. A double raise suggests a slam to partner, and you should avoid making such suggestions with a hand that has no slam value. For example, after partner opens one spade, change your hand to:

83. ♠ Q J 5 2   ♡ Q   ◇ Q J 9 3 2   ♣ Q J 10

Bid two diamonds, not three spades. Avoid suggesting a slam without a single ace or king in your hand. And with:

84. ♠ K Q J 2   ♡ Q   ◇ Q J 9 3 2   ♣ Q J 10

Bid three spades, but get ready to sign off if partner makes a slam try. If partner makes *two* slam tries, however, that will be another story.

A second good feature of Hand No. 82 is the strength of the trump support. Avoid a double raise with four *small* trumps or even with J-x-x-x. For slam purposes, partner usually needs something like Q-x-x-x or better.

85. ♠ 8 7 5 2   ♡ 4 2   ◇ A K J 9 3   ♣ K Q

Bid two diamonds, not three spades. If partner rebids the spades, you can jump raise to game. If his rebid is something else, you can take him to *three* spades.

A third good feature of Hand No. 82 is that the side strength is in more than one suit. If the side strength were concentrated in one suit, you could tell a more precise story by bidding that suit first and then raising the original suit vigorously.

86. ♠ K Q J 2   ♡ 4 2   ◇ A K Q 9 3   ♣ 6 2

Bid two diamonds, not three spades. Jump to four spades at your next turn.

The double raise shows a strong, but limited hand. When the hand is strong enough for a jump takeout in a new suit, don't be content with a mere double raise.

87. ♠ K J 5 2   ♡ 4   ◇ A Q 9 7 3 2   ♣ A 3

Bid three diamonds, not three spades. Here you envision a slam in spades even opposite a minimum opening bid. The jump takeout will stimulate partner if he has a diamond fit; a mere raise to three spades would give him nothing to get excited about.

The examples are, of course, carefully selected to illustrate the point. In actual play you sometimes get a hand that contradicts itself. For example:

88. ♠ 8 7 5 2   ♡ 4   ◇ A K J 9 3   ♣ K Q 3

The spades are very small, but the side strength is well divided between diamonds and clubs, and the singleton in the fourth suit is nothing to sniff at. Since the diamonds are only a small part of the story, you must raise to three spades despite the weakness of the trumps.

Similarly:

89. ♠ K Q J 2   ♡ 4   ◊ A K J 9 3   ♣ 5 3 2

The high-card strength is all in spades and diamonds, but a singleton heart is an essential part of the story. A jump to three spades is therefore better than a takeout to two diamonds.

The double raise in a *minor* suit, as we have already observed with Hand No. 72, should be avoided when any other informative response is available. The double raise should therefore promise not only the usual trump support and total strength, but also no other biddable suit. For example, in response to one diamond:

90. ♠ K 9 3   ♡ 4 2   ◊ A J 9 3 2   ♣ A Q 5

Bid three diamonds. No other response is available.

91. ♠ K 9 3   ♡ K 2   ◊ A J 9 3 2   ♣ Q J 5

Bid two notrump. A raise to three diamonds would not be *bad,* but the jump in notrump is better because if the hand has to be played at notrump you want the opening lead coming *up to* one of your kings rather than *through* it.

THE TRIPLE RAISE

The raise of a major suit from one to four shows great playing strength but no more than 9 points in high cards. The hand almost invariably includes five or more trumps and a singleton or void suit.

92. ♠ K J 8 7 4   ♡ Q 10 6 5 3   ◊ 5   ♣ 7 3

Raise to four if partner opens with either one heart or one spade.

The triple raise is intended to shut the opponents out and to warn partner away from a bad slam. If the opening bidder has a good enough hand, he may go past game, but he must be prepared to find such a dummy as Hand No. 92.

93. ♠ K Q 8 7 4   ♡ K Q 6 5 3   ◊ 5   ♣ 7 3

Raise to three if partner opens with either one heart or one spade. With 10 points in high cards, you are too strong for a raise to four

94. ♠ K Q 8 7 4   ♡ K J 8 6 5 3   ◊ 5   ♣ 3

Bid the other major if partner opens with one heart or one spade. Your next bid will be game in the original suit. Even though you have only 9 points in high cards, the hand is too strong for a mere triple raise. You must hit upon some way of encouraging partner to try for a slam if he has little more than three bare aces.

95. ♠ Q 8 7 4   ♡ K J 8 6 5 3   ◊ 5   ♣ 7 3

Bid two hearts in response to one spade. Avoid the triple raise with only four trumps if there is some reasonable chance of finding a better game contract. If partner opens with one heart, however, raise to four hearts.

96. ♠ 7 5 3   ♡ K J 8 6 5 3   ◊ 5 2   ♣ 7 3

In response to one heart, bid only two hearts. The hand is simply not strong enough for a triple raise. With a good partner, my own response would be one spade! When a hand is too weak for a triple raise in a major suit, you must always fear that the opponents have a game. If you can "steal" the other major, you get out with a whole skin. You intend, of course, to steer the bidding back to partner's suit.

The triple raise in a *minor* suit is practically non-existent. If, once in ten years, you get a hand that seems to call for so extreme an action, you won't need a book to tell you what to do!

THE ONE-OVER-ONE RESPONSE

The one-over-one response may be made in any biddable suit when no better response is available and when the count of the hand is anywhere between 6 and 17 points.

So much for the general rule, which is, of course, familiar to all experienced players. Let's look first at a few exceptions.

As we have already seen, with Hand No. 69, you don't bother to bid one spade in response to one heart if you can raise to two hearts. When a hand is worth only one response, your first duty is to raise a major suit.

Much the same is true when the hand is worth a *double* raise. Assume partner bids one heart, and that you hold:

97. ♠ A Q J 5   ♡ K 10 8 4   ◇ 6 2   ♣ K 9 5

Bid three hearts, not one spade. The spades are only part of the story; the double raise tells it all.

We have also seen that the biddable suit is preferred to a raise of a *minor* suit; and even to a double raise of a minor.

Occasionally, the choice is between a one-over-one response and a response in notrump. Partner bids one diamond, and you hold:

98. ♠ J 9 3 2   ♡ A Q 4   ◇ 8 3 2   ♣ J 7 4

One notrump is about as good a response as one spade. If the spades were stronger, you'd prefer to bid the suit; and you'd certainly show a *five*-card suit. If the spades were weaker, you'd surely prefer to bid one notrump. If the hand had some distributional advantage, you might prefer the suit response. The actual hand is a borderline case. (Many experts, particularly those who open only five-card or longer major suits, insist on responding in *any* four-card suit, even 5-4-3-2.)

Similarly, once again in response to one diamond:

99. ♠ J 9 3 2   ♡ A Q 4   ◇ Q 3 2   ♣ A J 7

Bid two notrump rather than one spade. You tell your whole story, very accurately, in one response. If you show only the spades, you have told only a very small part of your story — and a misleading part, at that.

Occasionally the one-over-one response dips below 6 points

or goes above 17 points. For example, in response to partner's bid of one club, you hold:

100. ♠ J 5 3 2   ♡ Q 9 5 3   ◇ J 9 8 6   ♣ 2

Bid one diamond. You expect to pass partner's next bid. The chances are that you will be better off than at one club. No guarantee goes with this sort of response. Your partner's next bid may be a jump to *three* clubs, or something equally revolting. Nevertheless, in the long run you will profit by responding with this sort of hand.

Similarly, in response to one club:

101. ♠ A J 6 5 3 2   ♡ A K 5   ◇ A K 4   ♣ 2

Bid only one spade. You have no support for clubs, and your own suit is quite shabby. You will get more information if you avoid the immediate jump.

When you have a reliable partner, you can sometimes afford to respond in an unbiddable suit. In response to one club:

102. ♠ 9 6 3 2   ♡ 9 8 5 4   ◇ K Q 4   ♣ A 2

Bid one diamond. If partner rebids in either major, you will raise. If he raises diamonds, you'll probably have to pass, but nothing is lost since the hand had no real future anyway.

Similarly, in response to one diamond:

103. ♠ 8 3   ♡ K J 4   ◇ 3 2   ♣ Q J 7 6 3 2

A response of one heart is about as good as one notrump. If partner's rebid is one notrump, the hand will be played from the more advantageous side. If partner's rebid is one spade, you can then bid one notrump. If he raises hearts with only three-card support, you are in trouble. Hence this sort of response must be avoided with flighty partners.

Another case, in response to one heart:

104. ♠ 7 5   ♡ Q J 8 5 4   ◇ K 8 3   ♣ 9 7 6

Bid one spade, not two hearts! You should be able to get back to hearts at any level. This is your best chance to "steal" the hand from the higher-ranking spade suit. Not recommended with flighty partners, but far safer than it looks with any partner of reasonable discretion.

When you have a choice of suits, your general rule is to respond in the *longer* of two biddable holdings:

105. ♠ Q 8 7 5 4   ♡ A K 6 3   ◇ 5 2   ♣ 6 3

In response to one club or one diamond, bid one spade. You can show the hearts next.

106. ♠ 5 2   ♡ A K 6 3   ◇ 6 3   ♣ Q 8 7 5 4

In response to one diamond, bid one heart. The hand is not strong enough for a response of two clubs.

With two four-card suits, make the stepwise (cheapest) bid:

107. ♠ K J 7 5   ♡ Q 8 6 3   ◇ 7 6   ♣ K J 6

In response to one club or one diamond, bid one heart. If partner then bids spades, you can raise; and if he raises hearts, you will be equally well off. The point is that you can try for *both* major suits with one response. If, instead, your first response is one spade, partner might have to suppress a four-card heart suit, and you likewise might never get around to showing your weak heart holding. You might thus miss the best trump suit.

If this stepwise principle is followed, a failure to make a stepwise bid indicates a *five*-card suit. For example:

South	North
1 ◇	1 ♠
1 NT	2 ♡

North has at least five spades. If he had four cards in each major, he would show hearts first. If he had five hearts and four spades, he would show hearts first. Hence he must have at least five spades; the hearts may be only four cards in length.

THE TWO-OVER-ONE RESPONSE

The non-jump 2-over-1 response is made with about 10 to 17 points and usually shows a good, playable suit.

108. ♠ 8 7 3   ♡ 9 6 4   ◊ K 9   ♣ A K 9 6 2

Bid two clubs in response to an opening bid in any of the other three suits.

The chief function of the 2-over-1 response is to show a strong hand. Don't mislead your partner with a strong bid when you have only a collection of queens and jacks:

109. ♠ Q 7 3   ♡ Q 6 4   ◊ K 9   ♣ Q J 9 6 2

In response to one diamond, bid only one notrump. The hand is simply not worth a 2-over-1 response because the true count is not really 10 points. In response to one spade or one heart, however, bid two clubs. Your queen of trumps can be upgraded, and you can assign a value to the doubleton in diamonds. The hand is worth substantially more than a single raise.

Occasionally, you must make a 2-over-1 response in a long, strong suit even though you have less than the proper count. You expect to rebid a minimum of your suit to indicate the nature of your hand:

110. ♠ 7   ♡ 8 2   ◊ 9 6 5 3   ♣ K Q J 9 6 2

In response to one spade, bid two clubs. You expect to bid three clubs at your next turn. This sequence is reserved for hands of this nature; you would find some other rebid if you really had the normal values for your bid.

The 2-over-1 response almost guarantees that you will make another bid at your next turn. You reserve the right to pass if your partner rebids two of his original suit or two notrump. If your partner rebids in a new suit, he expects you to bid again unless you had the one-suited bust illustrated in Hand No. 110.

THE JUMP IN A NEW SUIT

The jump takeout in a new suit is usually made on hands of 18 points or more. The point of the bid is to *suggest a slam* at the earliest possible stage of the bidding.

111. ♠ K Q 8 3   ♡ 9   ◇ A Q J 9 5   ♣ A 7 3

Bid three diamonds in response to one spade. A slam is quite probable, even if partner has only a minimum opening bid. Bid only two diamonds in response to one heart; slam is far from likely unless partner can show a diamond fit. Bid only one diamond in response to one club; you will show slam ambitions only if a real suit fit becomes clear.

112. ♠ 8 3   ♡ 9   ◇ A K Q J 9 5 2   ♣ A Q 3

Bid three diamonds in response to one spade or one heart. You intend to try for a slam in diamonds. You don't need a fit with partner's suit since you have an independent suit of your own.

113. ♠ Q 8   ♡ K 9 2   ◇ A K J 9 5   ♣ A Q 7

Bid three diamonds in response to one spade. You cannot guarantee a trump suit good enough for slam, but you are willing to fall back on notrump. You can jump to three diamonds over an opening bid of one heart, or two diamonds over one club, even though the spades are a bit weak for notrump.

114. ♠ K Q J 5   ♡ 8 3   ◇ K Q J 9   ♣ K Q J

In response to one spade, bid only three spades, not three diamonds. Avoid making a jump takeout with balanced distribution and no aces. Change the three of hearts to the three of diamonds, and you might have to bid three diamonds to do justice to the hand.

115a. ♠ K Q 9 3   ♡ 8   ◇ A Q J 9 5 3 2   ♣ 3

Bid three diamonds in response to one spade. Although you

have only 12 points in high cards, a slam in spades is a distinct possibility, even if partner has a minimum opening bid.

115b. ♠ K 3   ♡ K 9   ◇ A J 7 5 3 2   ♣ A K 7

Bid only two diamonds in response to one heart or one spade. You cannot guarantee a slamworthy trump suit, and you are not eager to fall back on notrump with two doubletons. A non-jump response will get you more information than a jump bid, and you can decide later on whether or not to try for a slam.

THE RESPONSE OF ONE NOTRUMP

The response of one notrump to an opening bid of one in a suit shows about 6 to 10 points, reasonably balanced distribution, and no suitable 1-over-1 response.

We have already seen cases in which the response of one notrump is compared with a single raise (Hands No. 73 to 76); with a 1-over-1 response (Hands No. 98 and 103); and with a 2-over-1 response (Hand No. 109).

Only two other situations remain to be covered: the response of one notrump to the opening bid of one club, and the choice between a response of one notrump and a pass.

After an opening bid of one club, a response of one notrump by-passes all responses and rebids at the level of one. Following the general principle that you need strength for a bid that cuts out bidding room, the response of one notrump to one club is pegged at 9 to 11 points with balanced distribution and no desirable 1-over-1 response available.

116. ♠ K 8 5   ♡ Q 7 4   ◇ J 7 3 2   ♣ A 9 3

Bid one notrump in response to one club.

117. ♠ K 8 5   ♡ A 7 4   ◇ J 7 3 2   ♣ A 9 3

Bid one diamond in response to one club. Too strong for a response of one notrump.

118. ♠ K 8 5 ♡ Q 7 4 ◊ J 7 3 2 ♣ J 9 3

Bid one diamond in response to one club. Too weak for a response of one notrump.

119. ♠ K 8 5 3 2 ♡ A 7 ◊ J 7 3 ♣ Q 9 3

Bid one spade in response to one club. Don't neglect to show a good five-card major suit.

120. ♠ K 8 5 ♡ Q 7 4 ◊ J 7 3 ♣ J 9 3 2

Bid one diamond or two clubs, in response to one club. The hand is too weak for a response of one notrump. One diamond should be preferred with a sensible partner.

When your choice is between one notrump and a pass, don't strain too hard to find a bid. This is particularly true when you are very short in partner's suit; a quick pass may keep you out of serious trouble.

121. ♠ 4 ♡ 8 3 2 ◊ K 9 7 6 2 ♣ J 6 3 2

In response to one spade, pass. The hand has no future.

122. ♠ 8 3 2 ♡ K 9 7 6 2 ◊ 4 ♣ J 6 3 2

In response to one spade, bid one notrump. If partner's rebid is two spades, you can pass; if he bids two clubs or two diamonds, you can take him back to two spades. However, if he bids two hearts you will then raise to three hearts, and hope for a game!

An important point to remember when you are considering a pass is that most opponents have no exact way of showing their strength when they reopen the bidding in this situation. Let's say the auction begins:

South	West	North	East
1 ♠	Pass	Pass	Double

West usually doesn't know the nature of East's hand. When West responds, East doesn't know the nature of West's hand. Guesswork often takes the place of system.

This auction is, however, very different:

South	West	North	East
1 ♠	Pass	1 NT	Double

Now East surely has a good hand. The East-West bidding can proceed on a sure footing.

For this reason, you sometimes make the bidding easier for the opponents when you make a doubtful response of one no-trump. Better to pass and let the opponents flounder.

THE RESPONSE OF TWO NOTRUMP

The response of 2 NT to an opening bid of one in a suit shows balanced distribution, stoppers in all of the unbid suits, and 13 to 15 points in high cards.

Experts and beginners use this bid in exactly the same way. The only possible refinement, perhaps, is that the expert avoids a response of 2 NT with a maximum holding of 15 points. A response in a suit may provide a better road to slam.

THE RESPONSE OF THREE NOTRUMP

The response of 3 NT to an opening bid of one in a suit shows balanced distribution, stoppers in all of the unbid suits, and 16 or 17 points in high cards.

This bid is a notorious slam killer. For this reason, most experts will not jump to three notrump with a *good* 17 points (especially if the hand contains two or more aces), or even with 16 points and a 5-card suit. Some experts refuse to use this response altogether.

RESPONSES BY A PASSED HAND

When your partner opens the bidding in third or fourth position, he knows that your hand counts to less than an opening bid. If his hand is a doubtful opening bid, or even a sound but minimum bid, he will be looking for a part score rather than for a game. He may therefore pass your response, whatever it may be.

When partner opens with a major suit for which you have a good three-card or better fit, you cannot afford to temporize by bidding a new suit. You cannot afford to risk a pass. Hence you must raise the major at once. If the hand is worth a raise to 2½, make up your mind whether to overbid or underbid — raise to three or to two, depending on the hand and your judgment. If the hand is worth a game opposite even a doubtful opening bid, raise all the way to four.

123. ♠ K 8 3   ♡ 9 7 6 2   ◊ A Q 9 4   ♣ 8 3

In response to one spade, raise to two spades. The hand is worth no more.

124. ♠ K J 8 3   ♡ 9 7 6 2   ◊ A Q 9 4   ♣ 3

Raise one spade to three spades. This would be a slight overbid except for the fact that you have passed originally.

125. ♠ K J 8 3   ♡ 9 7 6   ◊ A Q J 9 4   ♣ 3

Raise one spade to four spades. There will probably be a reasonable play for game even if partner has a minimum opening bid. If you raise to only three spades, he may pass.

The jump takeout by a passed hand is forcing for one round. It should show a maximum pass with a good fit for the suit named in the opening bid. It is this fit that makes your hand look so good even though it wasn't worth an opening bid.

126. ♠ K J 8 3   ♡ 7 6   ◊ A Q J 9 4 2   ♣ 3

Bid three diamonds in response to one spade, but only two diamonds in response to one heart. You are willing to be in game opposite a minimum spade bid, and you are willing to suggest a slam if partner has extra values. Opposite a heart bid, however, you cannot tell much about the future of the hand.

When your partner has opened in third position, avoid making a jump response of two notrump. Remember that he may have opened with somewhat less than a normal bid. If you do bid 2 NT, make sure that you have a maximum pass with several tens and nines. It's seldom fatal when one member of the partnership overbids, but often is when both partners overbid.

There is less objection to a response of 2 NT when your partner opens in *fourth* position. The chances are that he has a reasonably sound opening bid.

There is no such thing as a response of *three* notrump when your partner opens in third or fourth position. The only logical meaning is that you misread your hand the first time and that you have just discovered an extra ace lurking behind another card.

QUIZ No. 4

Partner has dealt and bid one club and the next hand has passed. What do you respond with each of these hands?

127.	♠ A 6 2	♡ K 5 2	◇ 9 7 6 4 2	♣ J 5
128.	♠ 7 2	♡ K Q 10 4	◇ J 7 4	♣ Q J 7 2
129.	♠ J 9 5 2	♡ K 7 3	◇ K 10 3	♣ K 5 4
130.	♠ K 7 6 2	♡ 7 5 4 2	◇ 8 2	♣ 7 3 2
131.	♠ A K 7 4 2	♡ 5	◇ A Q J 5	♣ Q 10 3
132.	♠ K 5	♡ 7 2	◇ K Q 7 4	♣ A Q 8 5 2
133.	♠ K 10 5	♡ K J 4	◇ A Q 9 4	♣ J 10 5
134.	♠ 5	♡ A K Q J 5 4	◇ K Q 7	♣ K 6 2
135.	♠ 10 8 5 3 2	♡ K Q 4	◇ K J 6	♣ 10 5
136.	♠ K Q 10 5 2	♡ A J 10 7 4 2	◇ 7	♣ 4

QUIZ No. 5

Partner has dealt and bid one heart and the next player has passed. What do you respond with each of these hands?

137.	♠ A 6 4 2	♡ Q 10 3 2	◇ 9 6 3	♣ 8 6
138.	♠ 10 7 4 2	♡ J 5	◇ Q 7 4 2	♣ 9 6 3
139.	♠ J 5 2	♡ J 7 4 2	◇ K 6 4	♣ 10 5 2
140.	♠ 7 2	♡ K 9 6 2	◇ A 10 4	♣ Q J 5 4
141.	♠ 7 2	♡ K 9 6 2	◇ 5 2	♣ A 10 8 4 2
142.	♠ K 7 4	♡ 5 2	◇ K 5 2	♣ Q 10 6 4 2

143.	♠ 8 4	♡ K 8 2	◇ K Q J 4 3	♣ 7 4 2
144.	♠ K Q 5 2	♡ Q 10	◇ A Q J 7 2	♣ 7 4
145.	♠ A 4 2	♡ 7 4	◇ 3	♣ A K Q 10 8 5 2
146.	♠ 8	♡ K J 4 3 2	◇ 7 4	♣ K 8 4 3 2

QUIZ No. 6

Partner has dealt and bid one spade and the next player has passed. What do you respond with each of these hands?

147.	♠ Q 9 2	♡ 10 2	◇ 10 9 2	♣ K Q 8 3 2
148.	♠ K J 5 2	♡ 5	◇ A 5 2	♣ Q J 7 4 2
149.	♠ Q 7 4 2	♡ 6 4	◇ 8 4 3 2	♣ 8 7 4
150.	♠ J 7	♡ Q 7 4 2	◇ K 7 4 2	♣ 8 4 2
151.	♠ J 4 2	♡ A 5 2	◇ 7 4	♣ K Q 10 9 2
152.	♠ 7 4	♡ A 5 2	◇ J 4 2	♣ K Q 10 9 2
153.	♠ K 4 2	♡ A 5 2	◇ Q 2	♣ J 7 6 4 3
154.	♠ ——	♡ 7 4 2	◇ 8 4 3 2	♣ K J 10 8 7 2
155.	♠ K 7 4	♡ 4	◇ 8 4 2	♣ K J 10 8 4 2
156.	♠ K J 4	♡ 8 4	◇ Q 10 7 4	♣ A 9 5 4
157.	♠ K 5 4	♡ Q J 4	◇ A 10 2	♣ K Q J 4
158.	♠ Q 10 7 5 4 2	♡ A K 5	◇ 4	♣ A 5 4

QUIZ No. 7

Your partner has opened fourth hand with one spade and the next player has passed. What do you, as a passed player, bid with each of these hands?

159.	♠ 7 4	♡ K 4 2	◇ 9 6 3 2	♣ J 7 4 2
160.	♠ J 5 4 2	♡ 7 3	◇ Q 10 8	♣ A K 3 2
161.	♠ J 5 4 2	♡ 7 3	◇ Q 8	♣ A K 5 3 2
162.	♠ K 10 7 6 5	♡ K 5 4	◇ Q 9 3 2	♣ 5
163.	♠ A Q 10 2	♡ A 4	◇ J 10 9 3 2	♣ 8 2
164.	♠ A 5	♡ 6 2	◇ K 9 5 3	♣ K Q 7 6 2
165.	♠ K 9 5 3	♡ 6 2	◇ A 5	♣ K Q 7 6 2

3. Rebids
by the Opening Bidder

Your opening bid of one in a suit has a very wide range — from about 12 points to about 24 points. In your second bid you must try to narrow the range down. The method of doing so depends partly on the nature of the response your partner has made.

THE BIDDING LEVEL

The higher you push the bidding, the more strength you must have. We have already seen that a response at the level of two shows more strength than a response at the level of one. The same principle is true of rebids.

South	North
1 ♣	1 ♦
1 ♥	

This rebid takes place at the lowest possible level. South may have a near-minimum opening bid.

South	North
1 ♠	2 ♥
3 ♦	

This rebid takes place at a high level — the level of three. South needs substantially more than a minimum opening bid.

We see the same principle in the case of "reverse" bids.

REVERSE BIDS

When you bid two suits in the "normal" order, you show the higher suit first and the lower suit later. If you bid the lower suit first, you have bid the suits in *reverse* order.

A reverse at the level of one shows no unusual strength:

South	North
1 ♣	1 ♦
1 ♠	

South may have a minimum opening bid. It is still possible for North to bid or make a choice at a low level.

When you show your second suit at a higher level, you need greater strength:

South	North
1 ♣	1 ♠
2 ♦	

North may have to bid three clubs in order to show his choice. He has been driven to this level by South's reverse bidding.

The story is different if South bids in the normal order:

South	North
1 ♦	1 ♠
2 ♣	

North may pass or bid two diamonds to make his choice of South's suit. He has not been driven to a high level.

In each of these cases, North may have a poor hand. South should not drive the bidding up to a dangerous level unless he himself has a very good hand. To put it another way, the reverse shows a very good hand.

What do you need for a reverse? With a 6-5 two-suiter, you need little more than a minimum opening bid. With a 5-4 two-suiter, you need about 18 points in high cards — or a fit for partner's suit to make up for a missing point or two. If partner has shown a new suit at the level of two, you can afford to reverse with only about 16 points in high cards.

In many hands the problem of the reverse must be considered not at your second turn, but before you make your *first* bid. If you can't afford a reverse, you must make allowance for that fact in choosing your opening bid.

Choose the opening bid in the three hands that follow:

166. ♠ A Q J 4   ♡ A K 9 5 3   ◊ A 2   ♣ 7 5

The hand is strong enough for a reverse. Open with one heart. You can afford to rebid two spades even if partner's response is one notrump.

167. ♠ A Q J 4   ♡ A K 9 5 3   ◊ 3 2   ♣ 7 5

The hand is not strong enough for a reverse. Open with one spade, and show the hearts later. If partner eventually takes you back to spades, you will have to stay there.

168. ♠ K J 4 2   ♡ A K Q 5 3   ◊ 3 2   ♣ 7 5

The hand is not strong enough for a reverse, and the spades are weak. You don't want partner to take you back to spades when he makes a choice. Therefore open with one heart and give up the spade suit unless partner happens to bid it.

Is a reverse forcing? Only when both partners have shown strength.

South	North
1 ♡	1 NT
2 ♠	

Not forcing. North has not shown strength. South must jump to *three* spades if he wants to force. Nevertheless, North should strain to find another bid.

South	North
1 ♡	2 ◊
2 ♠	

Forcing. North has shown strength by responding at the

level of two. Even if North is shy a point or two, the combined assets ought to be enough for a game. (Once every ten years, North may pass with an extreme misfit.)

REBIDS AT THE LEVEL OF THREE

The reverse is strong, as we have seen, because it threatens to drive the bidding to the level of three. You *surely* need a strong hand if you actually bid three instead of just threatening to do so:

South	North
1 ♠	2 ♥
3 ♦	

South should have about 16 points in high cards with good distribution. With a magnificent fit, South may shade off a point or so; with a poor fit, or with poor distribution, South needs an extra point or two.

For example, take the bidding situation just described:

169. ♠ A K 9 7 3   ♥ Q 8   ♦ A Q J 5 4   ♣ 2

Bid three diamonds. 16 points in high cards, good distribution, and the makings of a fit for hearts.

170. ♠ A K 9 7 3   ♥ 2   ♦ A Q J 5 4   ♣ 8 5

Bid two spades at your second turn. Only 14 points, and no fit at all for hearts. You would have bid *two* diamonds if partner's response had been one notrump or two clubs; but you cannot afford to bid *three* diamonds.

171. ♠ A K 9 7 3   ♥ Q 8 5   ♦ A K 5 4   ♣ 2

Bid three diamonds. You will raise hearts next. You postpone the heart raise because you want to bid three suits. This is the standard way of indicating extreme shortness in the *fourth* suit.

FORCING AND NEAR-FORCING REBIDS

A jump rebid in a new suit is forcing to game:

South	North
1 ♥	1 ♠
3 ◇	

South's rebid would be equally forcing if North's response had been one notrump rather than one of a suit.

A jump rebid in the *same* suit is invitational — but not forcing — when the responder has not shown strength:

South	North
1 ♥	1 ♠
3 ♥	

South's rebid would be equally invitational if North's response had been one notrump rather than one of a suit.

The jump rebid in the same suit is forcing when the response has been made at the level of *two*:

South	North
1 ♥	2 ◇
3 ♥	

South's hand is not necessarily stronger, but North has promised a minimum of about 10 points. Hence the combined strength must be enough for a game.

A jump raise in responder's suit is not forcing:

South	North
1 ◇	1 ♥
3 ♥	

North is invited, but not forced, to bid again. If North does bid again, a game-forcing situation exists. For example, North might next bid three spades, and South might bid four diamonds, and both bids would be forcing. In short, North can decline the invitation to game by passing three hearts, but any bid at all is considered an acceptance of the invitation.

The situation is much the same after a jump to two notrump:

South	North
1 ♡	1 ♠
2 NT	

North is invited, but not forced, to bid again. Any bid at all is considered acceptance of the invitation. If North wants to stop below game he must pass two notrump.

If the responder has shown strength by responding at the level of two, a non-jump rebid in a new suit at the level of *three* is considered forcing. Similarly:

South	North
1 ♡	2 ♣
2 ♢	

North has shown strength by the response at the level of two. South almost surely has better than a minimum opening bid, even if his extra strength is only distributional. North should consider himself forced unless he has responded on a bad hand just to get out of hearts. For example:

174. ♠ 9 7 3　♡ ——　♢ 8 6 2　♣ K Q 9 7 4 3 2

North should get out while the getting is good.

When a suit has been bid and raised, a rebid in a new suit is forcing for one round:

South	North
1 ♡	2 ♡
3 ♢	

North must bid again. For all he knows, South may be void of diamonds.

South	North
1 ♡	2 ♡
3 ♢	3 ♡
3 ♠	

North must bid again, assuming South is trying for slam.

RAISING PARTNER'S SUIT

When you raise partner's 1-over-1 response to two, you show a minimum opening bid (13 to 16 points) with four-card or good three-card support for his suit. When you raise to *three*, you show a middling opening bid (a good 16 to 18 points) with good four-card support. When you raise to game, you show a strong opening bid (19 points or more) with good four-card support.

For example:

South	North
1 ◇	1 ♠
?	

175. ♠ K 8 5   ♡ 9 2   ◇ A Q J 7 3   ♣ A 4 2

Bid two spades. The irreducible minimum.

176. ♠ 9 8 5 2   ♡ 9   ◇ A Q J 7 3   ♣ A 4 2

Bid two spades. Another irreducible minimum, featuring distributional strength to make up for weakness in high cards.

177. ♠ K 8 5 2   ♡ 9   ◇ A K J 7 3   ♣ A 4 2

Bid three spades. Since this kind of raise often paves the way to a slam, avoid counting full value for scattered queens and jacks. Aces and kings should form the backbone of slammish bids.

178. ♠ K Q 5 2   ♡ 9 3   ◇ A K Q 7 3   ♣ A 4

Bid four spades. North will probably make four spades with even the weakest response. Don't issue a mere invitation when you can make the decision all by yourself.

A raise to 2½ of partner's suit can often be indicated by a temporizing bid in a new suit:

South	North
1 ◇	1 ♠
2 ♣	2 ◇
2 ♠	

179. ♠ K 8 5　　♡ 9　　♢ A Q J 7 3　　♣ A J 4 2

South can almost raise to *three* spades at his second turn, but he is one trump and about a point or so shy. If the temporizing bid of two clubs is passed, the hand has no future.

When partner's response is made at the level of *two*, your raise to three shows a good hand — about the same as the raise to 2½ just described. A jump raise to four shows an even better hand, usually indicating a hand that is just slightly too weak to make an immediate slam try.

For example:

South	North
1 ♠	2 ♡
?	

180. ♠ A K 8 5 2　　♡ K 7 3　　♢ A J 5　　♣ 4 2

Bid three hearts. This raise shows a limited hand, since you would jump to four hearts with a better hand, but it is virtually forcing nevertheless. Responder has shown a good hand, and the opener has shown better than a minimum bid.

181. ♠ A K Q 5 2　　♡ K J 7 3　　♢ K Q　　♣ 4 2

Bid four hearts. You want to be in game no matter how much North has shaded his response. If North has enough strength in the unbid suits to try for a slam, you can cooperate.

182. ♠ A K Q 5 2　　♡　K J 7　　♢ K Q 3　　♣ 4 2

Bid four hearts. You prefer good four-card support, but you will settle for good three-card support. Partner should have a five-card suit for his response.

THE REBID OF ONE NOTRUMP

The rebid of one notrump shows reasonably balanced distribution, at least one stopper in an unbid suit, and no more than 15 points in high cards.

Assume that you have opened with one heart, and that partner has responded with one spade:

183. ♠ 8 5   ♡ A K J 6   ◊ Q 10 7 3   ♣ K J 4

Bid one notrump.

184. ♠ 8 5   ♡ A K J 6   ♣ A 10 7 3   ◊ K J 4

Bid two diamonds. The hand is too strong for a rebid of one notrump. The rebid of two diamonds does not *guarantee* more than 15 points, but at least it leaves the possibility open.

After your rebid of one notrump, your partner can relax and pass with any balanced hand of less than 10 points. He knows that the combined total will not be enough for game.

THE NON-JUMP REBID OF TWO NOTRUMP

The non-jump rebid of two notrump shows a hand that would have bid *one* notrump over a response at the level of one: balanced distribution, at least one unbid suit stopped, and 13-15 points in high cards.

When you have opened the bidding with only 11 or 12 points in high cards on the strength of a good suit, don't make a rebid of two notrump. Rebid your suit.

When you have about 16 to 18 points in high cards, bid a new suit rather than two notrump.

With more than 18 points in high cards you can jump to *three* notrump or make a jump bid in a new suit.

THE JUMP REBID OF TWO NOTRUMP

The "book" value of a jump to two notrump is 19 or 20 points in high cards — a hand that was too strong for an opening bid of *one* notrump but not good enough for an opening bid of *two* notrump. *Practical* experts invariably shade this down to 18 points, and some will even shade it down to 17 points when the hand includes a fairly good five-card suit.

THE JUMP REBID OF THREE NOTRUMP

A *single* jump to three notrump is the same as a single jump to two notrump: 19 or 20 points according to the book, possibly shaded to 18 or even a good 17 points.

For example:

South	North
1 ♡	2 ◊
3 NT	

185. ♠ K J 2   ♡ A Q J 7 2   ◊ 9 2   ♣ A K 8

It would be wicked to bid less than three notrump!

A *double* jump to three notrump (over a 1-over-1 response) may show 21 points, or a solid suit with about 17 or 18 points.

For example:

South	North
1 ◊	1 ♠
3 NT	

186. ♠ 8 3   ♡ A Q 2   ◊ A K J 7   ♣ A K 8 3

Your hand may run as high as 22 points but lack the requisites for a two notrump bid. As in this case, the hand may lack a stopper in the suit bid by partner.

187. ♠ 7 3   ♡ K 9 4   ◊ A K Q J 8 5   ♣ A J 5

This hand will probably provide a good play for three notrump even if North has a very weak hand.

BIDDING A NEW SUIT

As we have seen, you show substantial extra strength when you bid a new suit at the reverse level or at the level of three. When you show a new suit at the level of one, you do not promise extra strength. When you show a new suit at the level of two (without reversing) you don't exactly promise extra strength, but you hint that you probably have some.

For example:

South	North
1 ♣	1 ♡
1 ♠	

South promises nothing. He may have a dead minimum opening bid.

South	North
1 ♡	1 ♠
2 ◊	

South probably has more than a minimum opening bid. With a dead minimum he would tend to bid two hearts or one notrump at his second turn. The extra strength may merely take the form of good distribution, as in a 5-5 two-suiter.

REBIDDING YOUR OWN SUIT

A simple rebid in your own suit shows that the suit is rebiddable and that no better rebid is available. You should have a minimum opening bid of about 13 points to a weak 16 points.

A jump rebid in your own suit shows that the suit is playable even opposite a singleton (a strong 6-card suit, or perhaps a 5-card suit headed by 100 or 150 honors). The strength of the hand should be 17 to 19 points when partner has responded at the level of one, but may be shaded down to about 16 points when partner has responded at the level of two.

Avoid rebidding your suit just because it is rebiddable. Sometimes it is better to show a new suit while the bidding is still low (particularly at the level of one). When partner's response is one notrump, it is wise to pass any balanced hand of minimum strength even though the suit is rebiddable. (It usually pays, however, to rebid a *six*-card suit.)

REBIDDING AFTER A RAISE

After partner's single raise, count him for about 7 points and add your own count. If the total is enough for game (26 points), bid it. If the total is about 24 or 25 points, make some invitational bid. If the total is less than 24 points, pass and take your part score.

For example, after partner raises your one heart opening to two:

188. ♠ 6 3   ♡ A J 9 7 2   ◊ K Q 8   ♣ A 3 2

Pass. You have 14 points in high cards together with an extra point or so for length in hearts. The combined count should come to about 23 points at most.

189. ♠ 6 3   ♡ A Q J 7 2   ◊ K Q 8   ♣ A 3 2

Bid three hearts. You have 16 points in high cards, together with an extra point or so for length in hearts. The combined total should be about 24 or 25 points. You invite partner to bid game if he has maximum values for his raise.

190. ♠ 6   ♡ A Q J 7 2   ◊ K J 8 5   ♣ A 3 2

Bid three diamonds. You invite a game and ask partner to think better of his hand if he has a fit for diamonds.

191. ♠ K 6   ♡ A Q J 7 2   ◊ Q 8 5   ♣ A 3 2

Bid two notrump. This sort of rebid often shows much the same as an opening bid of one notrump.

192. ♠ 6   ♡ A Q J 7 2   ◊ K J 8 5   ♣ A K 2

Bid four hearts. The combined total should be 26 points.

After partner's *double* raise in a major suit, go on to game with any minimum opening bid. Bid three notrump if you have balanced distribution and stoppers in all unbid suits, particularly if your suit is a four-carder.

If you have more than a minimum opening bid, try for a slam. Any bid in a new suit is a slam try. You have the values for a slam try if you can take an ace out of your hand and still have a sound opening bid. This can be shaded to a king if you have a singleton. (See Chapter 7.)

After partner's *triple* raise in a major suit, you should tend to pass. Partner has distribution, but very little strength in high cards. With 20 points or more, however, you may go on as follows:

With 3 aces and king or singleton in the fourth suit, bid a slam at once.

With 3 aces but no control in the fourth suit, try for a slam. A cue bid, showing one of the aces will probably work best.

With two aces and second-round control of the other two suits, bid four notrump (Blackwood Convention).

Otherwise give up the slam.

QUIZ No. 8

North	East	South	West
1 ♣	Pass	1 ♡	Pass
?			

What do you, North, bid on each of the following hands?

193. ♠ Q 10 5   ♡ 9 4   ◇ A J 7   ♣ A Q J 7 4
194. ♠ K J 10 7   ♡ A Q 5   ◇ 7 3   ♣ K J 9 6
195. ♠ A J 5 2   ♡ A J 6   ◇ 5 2   ♣ A Q 10 9
196. ♠ A 6 4   ♡ K J 6 2   ◇ 8   ♣ A K 10 4 2
197. ♠ J 10 6 2   ♡ 10 6 2   ◇ A J 4   ♣ A K 5
198. ♠ K Q 2   ♡ K Q 10 4   ◇ 3   ♣ A K 10 8 6
199. ♠ A Q   ♡ J 4   ◇ A J 10 3   ♣ A Q J 8 4
200. ♠ A K 5   ♡ K Q 10 4   ◇ 6   ♣ A K 10 8 6
201. ♠ A Q 6 4   ♡ 4   ◇ 6 4   ♣ A Q 9 4 3 2
202. ♠ A 9 4 2   ♡ 6   ◇ J 2   ♣ A Q 10 4 3 2
203. ♠ A K J 4   ♡ K 5   ◇ 6 4   ♣ A K Q 6 4
204. ♠ A Q 6   ♡ Q 7   ◇ K 4   ♣ A K J 10 6 4

QUIZ No. 9

	North	East	South	West
	1 ♡	Pass	2 ◇	Pass
	?			

205.	♠ 6 4	♡ A K J 9 6 4	◇ A 4	♣ K J 4
206.	♠ 7	♡ K Q J 9 6	◇ Q 4	♣ A K J 4 2
207.	♠ 7	♡ K Q 10 4 2	◇ 6 4	♣ A Q 9 4 2
208.	♠ 6 4	♡ A K 10 6 2	◇ K Q 5	♣ K 3 2
209.	♠ Q J 6	♡ A Q 10 5	◇ K 6 4	♣ K 3 2
210.	♠ 5	♡ K Q J 10 9 6 4 2	◇ 8 3	♣ A Q J
211.	♠ 4	♡ A Q 9 8 4 3 2	◇ K 2	♣ A 5 4

QUIZ No. 10

	North	East	South	West
	1 ♡	Pass	1 NT	Pass
	?			

212.	♠ K 6 5	♡ A Q 9 7 3	◇ 10 4	♣ A 6 3
213.	♠ Q 6	♡ A K J 6 2	◇ Q 10	♣ A Q 8 3
214.	♠ A K J 5 4	♡ A Q 10 7 4 2	◇ A	♣ 5
215.	♠ 3	♡ A K 10 6 4 2	◇ A Q 9 2	♣ Q 4
216.	♠ 6 4	♡ K Q J 10 8 3	◇ K 5	♣ A 6 4

QUIZ No. 11

	North	East	South	West
	1 ♡	Pass	2 NT	Pass
	?			

217.	♠ 6 5	♡ K Q 10 8 3	◇ J 6 4 2	♣ A Q
218.	♠ A 5	♡ K Q 6 4 2	◇ A Q 6 4	♣ K 5
219.	♠ K 7 3	♡ A Q 9 4	◇ A K 2	♣ K 4 2
220.	♠ A J 5 3	♡ K J 10 4 2	◇ A 6	♣ 6 4
221.	♠ K 10 2	♡ A Q 7 3 2	◇ J 7 4	♣ K 4

QUIZ No. 12

North	East	South	West
1 ♠	Pass	3 ♣	Pass
?			

222. ♠ A K J 7 3   ♡ 10 7   ◇ 8 4   ♣ A J 10 2
223. ♠ A J 10 4 2   ♡ K Q 4 2   ◇ K 6   ♣ 6 4
224. ♠ A Q J 6 4 2   ♡ 6   ◇ A K 6   ♣ J 6 4
225. ♠ A K Q 10 4 2   ♡ 6 2   ◇ K 7 4   ♣ 6 2
226. ♠ A J 7 3 2   ♡ K 4   ◇ A Q   ♣ 9 6 4 2

QUIZ No. 13

North	East	South	West
1 ♠	Pass	2 ♠	Pass
?			

227. ♠ A Q 9 6 4   ♡ A 6 4   ◇ Q 10 2   ♣ J 4
228. ♠ A K J 6 2   ♡ K 5   ◇ K J 10 6 2   ♣ 4
229. ♠ A Q 10 8 2   ♡ K Q J   ◇ 4 2   ♣ K J 2
230. ♠ A K 6 4 2   ♡ A 6   ◇ A J 10 3   ♣ K J
231. ♠ K Q 9 5 2   ♡ A K 10 7   ◇ K J 7   ♣ 6

QUIZ No. 14

North	East	South	West
1 ♡	Pass	3 ♡	Pass
?			

232. ♠ Q J 6 4   ♡ A Q 10 6 2   ◇ K 6 4   ♣ 5
233. ♠ A Q 6   ♡ A K J 4 2   ◇ 6   ♣ K J 7 4
234. ♠ K 8 2   ♡ K Q J 6 4 2   ◇ 7   ♣ A 4 3
235. ♠ A 10 4   ♡ K Q 10 5   ◇ J 7   ♣ Q J 6 4
236. ♠ K 4   ♡ A J 9 4 2   ◇ K 3 2   ♣ K 4 2

4. Rebids
by the Responder

At your second turn as responder, you usually know the value of your partner's hand to within a point or so, and you know quite a bit about his distribution. This information, together with your own hand, tells you whether you should be thinking about part score, game, or slam.

Your next job is to pass the word on to your partner. For this purpose you should know which bids are forcing, which are fairly strong, and which are weak.

FORCING AND NEAR-FORCING REBIDS

All jump rebids you make as responder are forcing unless you have clearly limited your strength.

South	North
1 ◇	1 ♡
1 NT	3 ♡

The jump to three hearts is forcing. This is not the same as the opening bidder's jump rebid in the same suit.

South	North
1 ◇	1 ♡
1 ♠	3 ◇ or 3 ♠

In theory, these jump raises may not be completely forcing. In practice, nobody ever passes such a raise.

South	North
1 ♡	1 NT
2 ◇	3 ♡

This jump is not forcing. North has clearly limited his strength by bidding one notrump at his first turn.

South	West	North	East
1 ♡	1 ♠	Pass	Pass
2 ◇	Pass	3 ♡	

This jump is not forcing. North has clearly limited his strength by passing at his first turn.

If the responder bids a new suit at the reverse level or at the level of three, he creates a game-forcing situation:

South	North
1 ◇	1 ♡
1 NT	2 ♠

The partnership is committed to game.

South	North
1 ♠	2 ♡
2 ♠	3 ◇

The partnership is, again, committed to game.

A bid in the fourth suit is forcing for one round:

South	North
1 ♣	1 ◇
1 ♡	1 ♠

Likewise:

South	North
1 ♣	1 ♡
1 ♠	2 ◇

Responder's bid in a new suit may be non-forcing if the opener has clearly limited his strength:

South	North
1 ♡	1 ♠
1 NT	2 ◇

Not forcing. North must jump to *three* diamonds to force.

South	West	North	East
1 ♡	Pass	1 ♠	2 ♣
Pass	Pass	2 ◇	

Not forcing. South has clearly limited his strength by passing. North must jump to *three* diamonds to force.

Experts disagree on one rebid by the responder in a new suit:

South	North
1 ♣	1 ♠
2 ♣	2 ♡

It is possible to play this change of suit as a force for one round, and most of the leading experts play it this way. It is equally possible to play it as non-forcing. Whatever your own preference may be, it's wise to know which way your partner plays it. If in doubt, treat your partner's bid as forcing; and, if you are the responder, make a jump bid in this situation to make quite sure that your partner treats it as a force.

A jump to two notrump is forcing to game:

South	North
1 ♣	1 ♡
1 ♠	2 NT

North should have the usual 13 to 15 points, balanced distribution and a sure stopper in the unbid suit:

237. ♠ 8 3   ♡ A Q 9 5 2   ◇ K J 8   ♣ A 6 2

A non-jump rebid of two notrump is not forcing:

South	North
1 ♡	1 ♠
2 ♣	2 NT

North should have 11 or 12 points and a sure stopper in the unbid suit. Nobody will hang him if he reaches down to a good 10 points or up to a poor 13 points. A typical hand:

238. ♠ K Q 7 3   ♡ J 4   ◇ K J 8 5   ♣ Q 7 3

A belated raise, as we have already seen, is not forcing:

South	North
1 ♡	1 ♠
2 ♡	3 ♡

South may pass with a bare minimum opening bid. North must jump to *four* hearts if he wants to make quite sure of game.

If the raise is belated enough, however, it is forcing:

South	North
1 ♡	1 ♠
2 ♣	2 ◇
2 NT	3 ♡

North has evidently planned to make three responses. Any hand good enough for three responses is good enough for game.

Similarly:

South	North
1 ♡	1 ♠
2 ♣	2 ◇
3 ◇	3 ♡

The belated support for hearts must be considered forcing.

This is not the case, however, when the responder finally has a preference squeezed out of him:

South	North
1 ♡	1 ♠
2 ♣	2 ◇
3 ♣	3 ♡

South has insisted on one of his suits, and North has shown his preference. This is not forcing.

NON-FORCING REBIDS

The non-forcing rebids constitute no problem to the experienced player. When the hand is clearly headed for a part score, you may pass at your second turn, you may bid one notrump, you may rebid your own suit, or you may show a preference for one of partner's suits.

Most of the routine situations are covered in the quizzes, which follow.

QUIZ No. 15

	North	East	South	West
	1 ◇	Pass	1 ♡	Pass
	1 NT	Pass	?	

	♠	♡	◇	♣
239.	6 5	K Q 7 4 2	J 4 3	10 3 2
240.	10 4	A Q 4 3	Q 10 5 3	K 7 3
241.	10 4	A Q 4 3	K 8 4 2	7 5 3
242.	J 4	A Q 10 3	Q J 5 2	K 9 3
243.	7 5 2	J 10 7 6 3	—	Q 8 6 3 2
244.	5	K Q J 8 3	8 7 3	K 6 5 4
245.	5 3	K Q J 8 7 3	Q 4	A 6 3
246.	5	K Q J 7 5 3 2	Q 4	A 6 3
247.	5	A Q J 4 3	Q 4	A J 10 5 2
248.	A Q 9 2	A K 7 5 3	9 3	6 4

QUIZ No. 16

	North	East	South	West
	1 ◇	Pass	1 ♠	Pass
	2 ♠	Pass	?	

	♠	♡	◇	♣
249.	K Q 8 6 3	7 2	J 4	A 10 8 2
250.	A 10 7 4 2	7 3	Q 6 2	K 8 2
251.	K Q 9 4	Q J 3	6 3	K 10 5 2
252.	K Q 9 4	K J 3	6 3	A Q 5 2
253.	A Q 8 4	J 10 3	6 4	8 5 2

QUIZ No. 17

	North	East	South	West
	1 ◇	Pass	1 ♠	Pass
	2 NT	Pass	?	

	♠	♡	◇	♣
254.	Q J 10 2	10 6 3	Q 10	Q 7 3 2
255.	K J 6 3 2	10 4 2	7 5	K J 4
256.	A Q 10 5 4 2	8 6	Q 4	K 10 6
257.	A J 8 6 2	5 4	8 2	A 7 5 2
258.	Q J 8 6 2	Q 9 4 2	8 2	7 5

QUIZ No. 18

	North	East	South	West
	1 ♡	Pass	1 ♠	Pass
	2 ◇	Pass	?	

	♠	♡	◇	♣
259.	A K J 9 3	10 4 2	9 3	A Q 2
260.	K Q J 8 6 3	7 2	A 4	J 9 3
261.	K Q J 8 6 3 2	7 2	A 4 2	3
262.	A 7 4 3 2	Q 10 5	K J 2	5 2
263.	K J 5 4 2	J 6	7 4	10 8 3 2
264.	A K 10 4	6 2	K J 2	9 7 4 2
265.	A K 5 2	5 4 2	Q 7 4	7 6 2
266.	A K Q 6 4	K Q 8	Q 2	9 5 2
267.	K 9 7 5 2	3	8 6 2	K J 6 2
268.	A Q 7 4 2	K 6 2	4	K Q 3 2

QUIZ No. 19

	North	East	South	West
	1 ♠	Pass	1 NT	Pass
	2 ◇	Pass	?	

	♠	♡	◇	♣
269.	J 6	Q 4 2	A 10 8 2	10 8 3 2
270.	Q 4	A J 3	K 9 8 3	9 7 3 2

271.	♠ 10 5	♡ K Q 2	◇ J 8 4	♣ K J 8 6 2
272.	♠ 9 6 4	♡ K 10 3 2	◇ K 5	♣ J 8 3 2

QUIZ No. 20

North	East	South	West
1 ♡	Pass	2 ♣	Pass
2 ♡	Pass	?	

273.	♠ K 5	♡ Q 10 3 2	◇ 7 4	♣ A J 7 4 3
274.	♠ 7 5	♡ K Q 9	◇ 8 2	♣ A K 10 5 3 2
275.	♠ A J 8	♡ Q 5	◇ 10 4 2	♣ A Q J 5 3

QUIZ No. 21

North	East	South	West
1 ◇	Pass	1 NT	Pass
2 ♡	Pass	?	

276.	♠ A 5 4	♡ 9 7 6 3	◇ 10 4	♣ Q J 4 2
277.	♠ 7 6 4 2	♡ J 6 3	◇ J 3	♣ A J 4 3
278.	♠ 8 5 3	♡ J 7 2	◇ 10 5 4	♣ A J 8 2
279.	♠ K Q 4	♡ J 6 3	◇ 10 4 2	♣ Q J 4 2
280.	♠ A 5 4	♡ J 7 6 3	◇ K Q	♣ 8 6 4 3

5. Notrump Bidding

All opening bids in notrump show *shape, stoppers,* and *size.*

The *shape* is always balanced distribution: 4-3-3-3, 4-4-3-2, or 5-3-3-2. Once in a blue moon, a player may bid notrump with a 6-3-2-2 distribution or a 5-4-2-2.

The *stoppers* consist of at least three suits stopped for an opening bid of one notrump. All four suits must be safely stopped for bids of two or three notrump. In theory, a player who bids one notrump with three suits stopped should have at least Q-x or x-x-x in the fourth suit. In practice, many players will risk a bid of one notrump with only J-x in the fourth suit.

The *size* is 16 to 18 points for one notrump, 22 to 24 points for two notrump, and 25 or 26 points for three notrump. There is a gap — 19 to 21 points — between one and two notrump. With a hand of that size, the player should bid one of a suit and make a jump bid in notrump at his next turn.

In *any* part score situation, you tend to open with one notrump on any balanced hand of 15 points (instead of the usual 16 to 18) and sometimes even 14 points. This encourages your partner to compete against the enemy if he has a broken 5-card suit since the nature of your bid promises him reasonable support for his suit.

THE STAYMAN CONVENTION

Practically all good players use some variation of the Stayman Convention for their exploration of game bidding after an opening bid of one notrump. A response of two clubs does not promise a club suit, but asks the opening bidder to show a biddable major suit if he has one. It is also possible to explore part-score possibilities, but the primary purpose of the Convention is to reach a game contract. Of the many versions of the Convention extant, the one shown here is the oldest, simplest and in many ways the best.

The response of two clubs should be based on a minimum of 8 points in high cards. Both partners agree to keep the bidding open until a contract of two notrump or three of a major is reached — or, with extra strength, longer.

281. ♠ K 8 3 2   ♡ Q 7 5 4   ◊ K 4   ♣ 9 6 3
Bid two clubs in response to one notrump. If partner can bid two of a major, you will raise to three.

282. ♠ K 8 3 2   ♡ A 7 5 4   ◊ K 4   ♣ 9 6 3
Bid two clubs in response to one notrump. If partner can bid two of a major, you will raise to game.

283. ♠ K 8 3 2   ♡ Q 7 5   ◊ A 4   ♣ 9 6 3 2
Bid two clubs. If partner bids two spades, you will raise to four spades. If partner bids two diamonds or two hearts, you will bid two notrump. If partner bids two notrump, you will raise to three notrump.

284. ♠ K J 8 3 2   ♡ A 7 5   ◊ 6 4   ♣ 9 6 3
Bid two clubs. If partner bids two spades, you will raise to four. If partner bids two hearts or two diamonds, you will bid two spades. This will show five or more spades, since you would not show a mere 4-card suit after partner has denied a holding of four or more spades. If partner's rebid is two notrump, you will likewise bid the spades — *three* spades.

The opening bidder cannot pass a response of two clubs. With a biddable major, he bids it. With two biddable majors, he bids spades first. Lacking a biddable major, he shows a minimum notrump (16 or a bad 17 points) by bidding two diamonds. With a good 17 or 18 points, a *maximum* notrump, he bids two notrump.

	South	North
	1 NT	2 ♣
	?	

285. ♠ A J 7 5   ♡ K 9 6   ◇ A Q 5   ♣ K 7 4

Bid two spades. You have been asked to show a biddable major suit, and you must do so. From your point of view, the hand will play better at notrump than at spades, but you have already told your story and must leave the rest to your partner's judgment.

286. ♠ Q 5   ♡ K J 6 2   ◇ A Q 5   ♣ A J 7 4

Bid two hearts. Once again, a simple answer to a simple question. This rebid of two hearts shows that you do *not* have a biddable spade suit; if you had *both* majors you would make your first rebid in spades.

287. ♠ A J 7 4   ♡ K J 6 2   ◇ A Q 5   ♣ Q 5

Bid two spades. With both majors, your first rebid is in spades. If partner is interested in hearts, he will find a way to give you another chance.

288. ♠ A Q 5   ♡ A K 4   ◇ Q 7 4   ♣ J 10 6 2

Bid two diamonds. This rebid does not promise a diamond suit but merely says that you have a minimum notrump (16 or a bad 17 points) and no biddable major suit.

288a. ♠ A Q 5   ♡ J 8 6 2   ◇ A K 4   ♣ Q 7 4

Bid two diamonds. Most good rubber bridge players will not show an *unbiddable* suit in this situation. They don't want to reach four of a very weak major since game in notrump is usually much safer with such hands. The minimum biddable suit in this situation is generally considered to be Q-x-x-x. Some experts will show J-10-x-x. (Some, in fact, will show any four-card holding at all.)

289. ♠ A Q 5   ♡ A K 4   ◇ Q 7 4   ♣ Q J 8 6

Bid two notrump. This rebid shows a maximum notrump (a good 17 or 18 points) with no biddable major suit.

290. ♠ K Q 5   ♡ K Q J   ◊ Q J 4   ♣ Q J 8 6

Bid two diamonds. With a 17-point hand, you must decide whether it is "good" or "bad." In this case you have no ace, no tens or nines, and a large number of overvalued queens and jacks. Treat the hand as a *minimum* notrump.

291. ♠ A J 5   ♡ A Q 9   ◊ K 10 4   ♣ Q J 8 6

Bid two notrump. This time your 17-point hand includes two aces, a ten, and a nine. You can afford to treat this hand as a *maximum* notrump.

The responder usually finds out everything he needs to know from the notrumper's first rebid. If he can see a clear fit in a major suit, he can raise to three or to four, as in Hands 281 and 282. If it is clear that there is no fit in a major suit, he can bid two notrump (with 8 points or a bad 9 points) or three notrump (with a good 9 points or more).

In one situation, the responder may be in doubt as to whether or not there is a fit in a major suit:

South	North
1 NT	2 ♣
2 ♠	?

South has already shown a biddable spade suit, but may or may not have biddable hearts as well. If North is ready to raise spades, he will do so without worrying about the hearts. If North is chiefly interested in notrump and has bid two clubs as a sort of smokescreen, he will bid two or three notrump without worrying about hearts.

But what will North do if he has game-going strength with 4-card support for hearts? How does he find out whether or not South has biddable hearts?

North must make a temporizing bid. He must keep the bidding open without getting past three notrump. A bid of three diamonds fits the bill, and North can afford to make this bid whether or not he has a biddable diamond suit.

For example, North would first bid two clubs and then three diamonds with such a hand as:

292. ♠ 7 5   ♡ K 8 6 5   ◊ 8 4   ♣ A Q 9 4 2

An experienced partner will be glad of the chance to bid three hearts if he has a biddable heart suit. If he lacks biddable hearts, he will bid three notrump. He will not raise diamonds, since he will not be sure that the bid of three diamonds really shows a suit.

One word of advice: Do not make this bid with an unreliable partner. Take your chance on three notrump and forget about delicate bids. If your partner is a bull, don't let him into the china shop.

What about using three *clubs* as a temporizing bid in this situation? Thus:

South	North
1 NT	2 ♣
2 ♠	3 ♣

The trouble is that many players use this sequence of bids — two clubs and then three clubs — to show a *club bust* — asking partner to pass before the opponents begin to double. For example:

293. ♠ 4 2   ♡ 7 3 2   ◊ J 4   ♣ Q J 7 5 3 2

This hand may not make three clubs, but you will probably fare better at that contract than at any number of notrump.

South may conceivably bid three notrump anyway, but he should have A-K-x of clubs to begin with, and a stopper in each of the other suits. Even then, he will probably go down. His best bet is to take a deep breath and pass. Part scores have their value too!

Some expert partnerships use an *immediate jump* to three clubs to show the club bust. Thus:

South	North
1 NT	3 ♣

This shows the sort of hand illustrated in No. 293.

This method is preferable when you are absolutely sure that your partner understands exactly what you mean by the bid. Do not risk it with a stranger, nor even with an old friend unless you have discussed the bid and made a firm agreement to use it.

The advantages of using a jump to three clubs to show a club bust are twofold:

1. You can begin with two clubs and later bid either three clubs or three diamonds as an exploratory bid. This gives you the chance to describe your hand accurately.

2. When you have a really bad hand, your jump bid helps to shut the enemy out. A player who might come in after a bid of two clubs may pass tamely after a jump to three clubs.

The temporizing bid of three diamonds (or, with a good partner, of three clubs) does not *necessarily* show an interest in an unbid heart suit. For example:

South	North
1 NT	2 ♣
2 ♠	3 ♦

294. ♠ K Q 9 3   ♡ 6 4   ◇ A Q 5   ♣ K J 8 4

With 15 points in high cards, North knows that the combined count is 31 to 33 points. Slam is a distinct possibility, and North can explore without demanding by bidding the diamonds and *then* raising the spades to game. This clearly suggests a slam since North would go right to four spades without saying a word about his diamonds if he were interested solely in game.

NON-STAYMAN RESPONSES

When you use the Stayman Convention, you don't give up the other responses — two of a suit (other than clubs), three of a suit, four of a suit, two notrump, and three notrump. These bids all have clear and normal meanings.

For example, assume that your partner has opened the bidding with one notrump. You would respond as follows:

295. ♠ K J 9 4 3 2   ♡ 7 4   ◇ 8 3 2   ♣ 8 5

Two spades. You will probably make a safe part score at spades. One notrump might be defeated.

296. ♠ K 9 4 3 2   ♡ J 7 4   ◇ 8 3 2   ♣ 8 5

Pass. There is no need to take partner out in a weak five-card suit when the hand is balanced. This hand is a borderline case. Make the spades a trifle stronger, and you would tend to take out; make them a trifle weaker, and you would surely pass. As the hand stands, you may either bid or pass.

297. ♠ K Q 9 3 2   ♡ Q 7 4   ◇ 8 3 2   ♣ 8 5

Bid two spades. This bid is not a rescue, since one notrump should be a safe contract. If partner has a maximum notrump and a spade fit, he will bid again; and then you will go to game. Otherwise, you will be satisfied with a safe part score.

298. ♠ 7   ♡ 8 5 4   ◇ 9 8 6 5 3 2   ♣ 7 4 2

Two diamonds. This is, of course, a bad hand. It will be good for three or four tricks of its own at diamonds, but will be quite worthless at notrump.

299. ♠ A Q J 9 4   ♡ 7 4   ◇ K 3 2   ♣ J 8 5

Three spades. You are ready to accept either three notrump or four spades as a final contract. If your long suit were a minor, you would raise immediately to three notrump without bothering to show the suit.

300. ♠ 7   ♡ A Q J 9 4   ◇ K Q 2   ♣ A J 8 5

Bid three hearts. You expect to reach a slam in hearts, clubs, or possibly notrump. Meanwhile, your first step is a jump in your best suit.

301. ♠ A J 9 4 3 2   ♡ 8   ◊ K 3 2   ♣ 6 5 2

Bid four spades. It would be pointless to jump to only three spades since you will not be satisfied with three notrump and have no interest at all in a slam. You confidently expect to make four spades.

302. ♠ Q J 9 7 4 3 2   ♡ 8   ◊ K 6 3 2   ♣ 2

Bid four spades. You haven't any idea of what you can make, since everything depends on how the hands fit and whether your partner has aces or K-Q combinations in hearts and clubs. In the long run it pays to bid such hands aggressively rather than timidly.

303. ♠ 9 4 2   ♡ K 4 2   ◊ A J 5   ♣ 10 9 8 3

Bid two notrump. With 8 points you can just barely invite partner to bid game. He will do so with a maximum notrump, but may pass with a minimum. It doesn't pay to extend this invitation with a *bad* 8 points. In this case, however, your jack is well placed and you have a ten and two nines to bolster up the hand.

304. ♠ 9 4 2   ♡ K 6 3   ◊ A Q 5   ♣ 6 5 3 2

Bid two notrump. Any 9-point hand is worth a raise.

305. ♠ 9 4 2   ♡ K 10 3   ◊ A Q 5   ♣ 10 9 8 4

Bid three notrump. Don't fail to reach game when you have a *good* 9 points or more.

306. ♠ 9 4   ♡ 10 6 3   ◊ 7 5   ♣ A Q J 8 4 2

Bid three notrump. The clubs will provide six running tricks if partner has the king (highly probable, since he has bid one notrump), and may even provide six tricks if he lacks the king. He needs little else to make game. A long suit headed by the ace is worth its weight in gold at notrump; the opponents cannot shut the suit out by means of a hold-up play.

307. ♠ 9 4 2   ♡ K J 3   ◊ A Q 5   ♣ K J 8 4

Bid three notrump. The combined count will be only 32 points even if partner has a maximum (18 points). Since slam is too unlikely to consider, especially with no long suit to run, there is no reason to beat about the bush. Partner can relax as he plays this hand.

308. ♠ K 9 5 3 2   ♡ K Q 4   ◊ 8 3 2   ♣ 8 5

Bid two clubs. With 8 points and a 5-card major, you are hovering between part score and game. You are too strong to bid a mere two spades, but not strong enough to bid three spades. You can suggest this in-between hand by using the Stayman response of two clubs as a starter. If partner shows spades, you will raise to four; if he bids two notrump, you will raise to three.

If partner now bids two hearts or two diamonds, you will bid two spades. The rebid of two spades indicates a 5-card suit (you already know that partner doesn't have biddable spades, so you wouldn't bother to show a mere *four*-card suit) and a willingness to reach game. If partner can raise spades (showing a good *three*-card fit), you will go on to game; but if partner bids two notrump, denying a good fit, you will pass.

RESPONDING TO TWO NOTRUMP

The opener shows 22 to 24 points.

With 0 to 3 points, pass.

With 4 to 8 points, choose a game contract.

With 9 or 10 points, suggest a slam.

With 11 or 12 points, insist on a small slam.

With 13 or 14 points, make sure of a small slam and suggest a grand slam.

With 15 to 18 points, insist on a grand slam.

The only way to stop under game is to pass the opening bid of two notrump. If you make any response at all, the partnership is committed to game.

If your first response is three clubs, this is, of course, *Stayman*. The opener is expected to show a biddable major if he has one; to bid three diamonds with minimum values and no major;

to bid three notrump with maximum values and no major. You, the responder, may be looking for either game or slam; it is up to you to make this clear as the bidding develops.

When you, as responder, have an unbalanced hand, you may insist on playing the hand at a suit contract. In general, it doesn't pay to do so with a minor suit unless you have enough strength in high cards (at least 8 points, even with an unbalanced hand) to think about a slam.

When your suit is a major, you can bid three and then four of your suit even with no strength at all. The hand will play better at your suit than at notrump. Sometimes the hand is doomed, but the loss is smaller at four of your major (at least 5 cards, usually more) than at notrump.

Experts do not agree on the meaning of this auction:

South	North
2 NT	4 ♡

Some think it means "Stop. This is a bad hand." Others think it means "Bid again. Slam is not sure, but is possible. We are safe at the level of five." In the majority of cases, it means nothing useful at all. The notrumper passes, and if slam is made, the responder can point to his jump bid and put the blame on his partner. If slam is not made, the responder says nothing at all.

In the ordinary rubber bridge game, don't use this jump response at all. If you have a favorite partner, discuss the situation and agree whether the bid should show strength or weakness. Either method is quite playable, provided that both partners know exactly what is meant.

A raise from two notrump to four notrump is, of course, a slam try. The opener is asked to go to slam with 24 points, but to pass with only 22. The responder should therefore have either 9 or a bad 10 points.

The responder can show slightly greater strength by bidding three of his suit first and then bidding four notrump. This should show 10 points or a bad 11 points. This is a dangerous auction in most games, since the opener may assume that the 4 NT bid is Blackwood and that he is forced (rather than invited) to rebid. If you don't want to take this risk, jump from two notrump directly to five notrump. This gives the opener the chance to get out if he has a minimum; he will bid six with anything more than a bare 22 points.

A direct leap from 2 NT to 6 NT should show 11 or 12 points without a long suit. With 13 or 14 points and a 5-card suit, you can hint at the grand slam by bidding the suit first and then jumping to six notrump. It is clear that you could have bid six notrump at your first turn, and that you took time out to bid the suit only in order to suggest a grand slam.

RESPONDING TO THREE NOTRUMP

The opener shows 25 to 27 points and is already in game. The responder should be willing to pass with balanced distribution and 0 to 6 points.

If the responder acts at all, it will be assumed that he is considering a slam or that he has a long suit and unbalanced distribution, in which case slam may still be a strong possibility.

With 7 points or more, the responder is willing to embark on a slam auction. This may likewise be true if the responder has a long suit and about 5 or 6 points in high cards. If the responder has less, he bids at his peril.

A response of four clubs is Stayman, but the responder should avoid this response unless he has a very strong preference for a major-suit contract (at least 9 cards in the major suit), or unless he can afford to make further moves towards a slam.

THE OPENING BID OF TWO CLUBS

Many experts use the opening bid of two clubs to show a very powerful notrump hand. This is treated much like a forcing opening bid of two in a suit, except that the negative response is two diamonds. *Any* other response shows strength.

The opening bidder makes a minimum rebid in notrump (usually 2 NT is enough) to show that his bid was a maximum 2 NT — balanced, all suits stopped, and 23 or 24 points.

The opening bidder makes a jump rebid in notrump (usually 3 NT) to show that his bid was the average player's opening bid of 3 NT — balanced, all suits stopped, and 25 or 26 points.

This leaves the opening bids of 2 NT or 3 NT available for other duties. The usual procedure is to bid 2 NT with only 21 or 22 points, and the right stoppers and shape. The opening bid of 3 NT may safely be ignored. (Some experts like to use this bid for the long solid minor suit with a smattering of kings and queens on the side — a "gambling" bid.)

This use of the opening bid of two clubs may be combined with ordinary strong two-bids in the other suits. Many experts combine it with *weak* two-bids in the other suits. In Europe, it is usually combined with invitational but not forcing two-bids in the other suits.

Any of these methods is quite playable, provided that you and your partner know exactly what is meant. Don't dream of springing any such bid unannounced and undiscussed in the average rubber bridge game — even with your favorite partner.

QUIZ No. 22

What do you bid as dealer with each of the following hands?

309. ♠ A 3   ♡ K J 6 4   ◇ Q 9 3   ♣ A Q 5 4
310. ♠ A Q 10 3   ♡ K 5   ◇ A K J   ♣ A J 9 2
311. ♠ A J 10   ♡ K J 2   ◇ Q 10 9 3   ♣ K J 8
312. ♠ Q 7 4   ♡ A J   ◇ K J 3   ♣ A Q 10 4 2
313. ♠ Q 10 9   ♡ K Q 10   ◇ A J 4   ♣ A K 10 4
314. ♠ A Q   ♡ A 4   ◇ K Q J 3 2   ♣ A K Q 8
315. ♠ K 10 6 3   ♡ A J 9 4   ◇ J 5   ♣ A Q J
316. ♠ K Q 10   ♡ A Q 5   ◇ A K J 4 2   ♣ A J
317. ♠ Q 10 2   ♡ A 10   ◇ K Q 4 2   ♣ A Q 10 3

QUIZ No. 23

	North	East	South	West
	1 NT	Pass	?	

318. ♠ Q 8 7 4 3   ♡ J 5   ◇ 10 7 4   ♣ 9 8 2
319. ♠ K 10 9 8 6 4 3   ♡ 8   ◇ 10 5 2   ♣ K 5
320. ♠ 8 7 6 2   ♡ K 10 6 3 2   ◇ 4   ♣ J 9 2
321. ♠ Q 10 4 2   ♡ 7 3   ◇ A Q 4   ♣ Q J 3 2
322. ♠ 10 7 4 2   ♡ 8 3   ◇ 5   ♣ A Q J 9 7 4
323. ♠ K 10 3   ♡ J 9 4 2   ◇ Q 10 4   ♣ K J 3
324. ♠ A K J 9 6 3   ♡ Q 4   ◇ 7 5   ♣ 8 3 2
325. ♠ Q 6   ♡ K 10 9 7 2   ◇ K 8 6 2   ♣ 9 2
326. ♠ 8 5   ♡ A Q 8 7 6 4   ◇ 7 5   ♣ 10 8 3

QUIZ No. 24

	North	East	South	West
	2 NT	Pass	?	

327. ♠ 9 8 6   ♡ Q 4   ◇ Q 7 5 2   ♣ J 4 3 2
328. ♠ Q 5 2   ♡ 8 4 2   ◇ J 7 4 3   ♣ 9 5 4
329. ♠ A Q 5   ♡ J 4   ◇ K 7 4 3 2   ♣ 9 7 6
330. ♠ 4 2   ♡ K 10 7 5   ◇ K 6 3   ♣ 10 5 4 2
331. ♠ A Q 5   ♡ Q 4   ◇ K 10 8 3   ♣ 10 6 3 2

QUIZ No. 25

	North	East	South	West
	1 NT	Pass	2 ♣	Pass
	?			

332. ♠ 10 9 4 3   ♡ A Q J   ◇ K J 4   ♣ K Q 3
333. ♠ K J 5   ♡ A Q   ◇ K J 9 3   ♣ A 9 6 4
334. ♠ A J 7 4   ♡ K Q J 5   ◇ A 10 3   ♣ K 5
335. ♠ A 9 7 6   ♡ K Q 10 5   ◇ A 10 3   ♣ K 2
336. ♠ A Q 5   ♡ Q J 3 2   ◇ K Q 9 2   ♣ A 10

QUIZ No. 26

North	East	South	West
1 NT	Pass	2 ♣	Pass
2 ♦	Pass	?	

337. ♠ Q 9 7 2   ♡ 5 3   ♦ A J 4 2   ♣ Q 8 2
338. ♠ K 10 8 2   ♡ 10 3   ♦ A J 7 2   ♣ Q 8 5
339. ♠ A Q 9 7 4 ♡ Q   ♦ K 10 3   ♣ 10 6 4 2
340. ♠ 5   ♡ Q 7 4 2   ♦ 8 4   ♣ A Q 10 9 6 3
341. ♠ 10 2   ♡ 8 7 4 3   ♦ 5   ♣ K 10 8 6 4 3

QUIZ No. 27

North	East	South	West
1 NT	Pass	2 ♣	Pass
2 NT	Pass	?	

342. ♠ K 4   ♡ Q 3   ♦ K Q 7 4 3   ♣ A 10 8 2
343. ♠ J 9 7 3   ♡ A Q 10 6 2 ♦ 7 4   ♣ K 5
344. ♠ Q 10 7 3   ♡ A 9 6 5   ♦ 9 3 2   ♣ Q 2
345. ♠ 8 6 4   ♡ 9 7 3   ♦ 4   ♣ A J 10 4 3 2

QUIZ No. 28

North	East	South	West
1 NT	Pass	2 ♣	Pass
2 ♡	Pass	?	

346. ♠ K 5   ♡ Q 10 3 2 ♦ Q 10 4 3 2   ♣ K 5
347. ♠ K 5   ♡ Q 10 3 2 ♦ J 9 6 4 2   ♣ Q 4
348. ♠ Q 10 4 3   ♡ K 8 3   ♦ J 5 3 2   ♣ Q 4
349. ♠ A K 7 6 2 ♡ Q J 4   ♦ 8 6 4 2   ♣ J
350. ♠ A K 7 6 2 ♡ J 5 4   ♦ J 6 2   ♣ K 3

6. Opening Shutout Bids

An opening bid of three or more in a suit is an attempt to shut the opponents out of the auction or to make it difficult for them to reach their best contract. Such bids are called *shutout*, or *pre-emptive* bids.

The shutout bid usually operates against your partner as well as against the opponents. Your partner will have few problems with a hand chock full of aces and kings or with any weak hand. You must avoid giving him a problem if his hand contains a few scattered high cards.

For this reason the typical shutout bid is based on a long suit with no outside high cards. In fact, even the suit itself is very rarely solid. The point is that the bidder's hand promises to take not a single trick on defense (his partner can double an opponent's bid only if he has the contract — and any possible rescue — beaten in his own hand), and that slam is very unlikely unless the responder can take care of all the side suits and can furnish a little help for the trump suit itself.

Before we look at an example, let's consider the factor of safety. It would be foolish to open with three of a suit, get doubled, and suffer a penalty of 1400 points. You wouldn't mind it a bit, however, if the penalty were only 200 or 300 points. Where is the dividing line? When do the tears begin to flow?

Nobody really knows. Beginners should base their shutout bid on the theory that they don't want to risk a penalty of more than 500 points, but experienced players can afford to be more enterprising.

The Rule of 500 Points (sometimes called the Rule of Two

and Three) prevents you from going completely overboard with your shutout bids. This rule provides that you need enough playing tricks in your own hand to come within two tricks of your bid when you are vulnerable, and within three tricks of your bid when you are not vulnerable.

If you follow this rule you will seldom be penalized more than 500 points. This is a good rule to expound to unreliable partners and to all opponents. Don't stick to it yourself, however, unless you can't trust yourself. (The beginning of wisdom is to know your own weaknesses.)

The real test of any bid is not what it will win or lose on any single occasion — but what it will win or lose *in the long run*.

Suppose, for example, that the opponents have a cold game, worth about 600 points. If you make a shutout bid and crowd them into bidding game in the wrong suit, you will be plus 100 instead of minus 600. This represents a gain of 700 points. You may even goad them into bidding an unmakable slam, and your gain will then be still larger.

Occasional triumphs of this sort, and they aren't so rare as you might suppose, make up for some of the big penalties you may run into. You can afford to go for 700 or even 800 points a fair portion of the time and still come out ahead of the game.

If the opponents in your particular game are slow to double or reluctant to let a double stand, you can be bold to the point of impudence with your shutout bids. The average player is far too fearful and stodgy to take full advantage of the possibilities of shutout bids.

Now let's see a typical shutout bid, not vulnerable against vulnerable opponents:

351. ♠ Q J 8 7 6 3 2   ♡ 8   ◊ 8 3 2   ♣ 7 6

Open with three spades in first, second, or third position. Once every ten years the opponents will double and take you for a real ride. The rest of the time they will stumble into good and bad contracts instead of bidding the hand normally and comfortably.

You would be reluctant to make the same bid with neither side vulnerable — you would prefer to have slightly better spots in spades or 7-4-1-1 distribution — but if this is what you are dealt, you should still bid three spades. Most experts make this kind of bid in high-stake games, and very few experts are practicing philanthropists!

When both sides are vulnerable, you need a higher safety factor. The opponents are more likely to let a double stand. A typical vulnerable bid of three spades:

352. ♠ K Q J 7 6 3 2   ♡ 8   ◊ 8 3 2   ♣ 7 6

Bid three spades with both sides vulnerable. You can expect to win only six tricks, but your trump suit is so strong that nobody can feel very happy about doubling you. If the hand belongs to the enemy, they will probably bid rather than double; and they will have far less bidding room than if you had passed.

You can afford to change the nature of your bid slightly in third position:

353. ♠ 7 5   ♡ 9   ◊ K J 8 6 4 3 2   ♣ A 4 3

Bid three diamonds. Since your partner has passed, game is very unlikely and slam is out of the question. The hand probably belongs to the enemy, and you can make life difficult for them by starting things off at the level of three. Moreover, if they eventually play the hand and must make a crucial play in clubs, they will probably mislocate the ace.

Shutout bids in the major suits often shut the opponents out. Three-bids in the minor suits are less likely to do so, but may do an equally effective job of crowding the enemy's bidding.

An opening bid of four should usually be considerably stronger than the three-bids we have been discussing, or should be based on fantastic distribution, such as 7-5-1-0. The opponents will often bid over your opening bid of *three,* but they will usually stand by a double of *four* when the hand clearly belongs to them.

354. ♠ 7   ♡ K Q J 8 6 4 3   ◇ Q J 7 5   ♣ 8

Bid four hearts. Even if doubled, you are likely to take eight tricks in the red suits. You may even make four hearts on a hand where the opponents are cold for four spades!

What about pre-emptive bids when you are vulnerable against non-vulnerable opponents? The simplest answer is that there is no such bid.

If your pre-emptive bids are enterprising in this situation, even the stodgiest of opponents will take time out to double for penalties. If your pre-emptive bids are not enterprising, what *should* they be?

With unfamiliar partners, don't make such bids at all. With your regular, trusted, partners, you may give a special meaning to the three-bid in unfavorable vulnerability: Such a bid should show an absolutely solid 7-card suit, inviting partner to bid three notrump if he can stop three suits and take two reasonably fast tricks in the process. For example:

355a. ♠ 7   ♡ 9 2   ◇ A K Q 10 7 5 3   ♣ 8 5 4

Bid three diamonds, vulnerable versus non-vulnerable — provided that your partner thoroughly understands the bid and knows what to do about it. (Incidentally, the opponents are likewise entitled to an explanation of this bid.)

RESPONDING TO A SHUTOUT BID

In order to respond sensibly to your partner's opening shutout bid, you credit him with a reasonably typical hand and thus determine whether or not the combined hands are good enough for a higher contract.

If your partner has opened with three of a suit, not vulnerable, you should not consider a game unless you have a hand that you would have opened with 1 NT (or more) as dealer. To put it another way, you need at least 16 points in high cards, including a reasonable fit for your partner's suit. This may be slightly reduced if you have a very good fit for partner's suit, particularly if you are short in some other suit. Conversely, you need considerably more than 16 points if you have a bad fit for partner's suit; he may have three losers in his own trump suit!

For example, suppose that partner has opened with three spades, not vulnerable against vulnerable opponents:

355. ♠ K 4   ♡ A 9 6 3   ◇ A Q 4   ♣ A 10 8 3

Bid four spades. There should be a reasonable play for this contract even if partner has some such miserable hand as No. 351.

356. ♠ 9 4   ♡ A K 6 3   ◇ K Q 4   ♣ A Q 8 3

Bid four spades. As your fit becomes worse, your outside strength must increase. This is an 18-point hand, and it is by no means a sure game opposite Hand No. 351.

357. ♠ 4   ♡ A K 6 3   ◇ K Q 5 4   ♣ A Q 8 3

Pass. Bid four spades if neither side is vulnerable, since partner may then have a slightly better hand than No. 351. Bid four spades very cheerfully if both sides are vulnerable. If partner is conservative enough to believe in the Rule of 500 Points, you may raise to four spades with this hand even when non-vulnerable against vulnerable opponents.

358. ♠ K 9 4 2   ♡ 3   ◇ K Q 5 4   ♣ A Q 8 3

Bid four spades. You can raise with fewer than 16 points when you have a good distributional fit for partner's suit.

359. ♠ 10 9 5 4   ♡ 3 2   ◇ K Q 9 5 4   ♣ 8 3

Bid four spades. Your partner announces that he has no defense, and you likewise are defenseless. The opponents must have a slam! Many experts would jump to five spades or to some such psychic spot as four notrump in the effort to talk the enemy out of their slam.

360. ♠ 5 4   ♡ K J 9 2   ◊ K Q 9 5   ♣ A J 3

Pass. This hand, with a poor fit and only 14 points, is not good enough to produce a game and is not bad enough to justify a further pre-empt. If you pass quickly and calmly enough, fourth hand may refuse to be shut out — and you will be delighted to hear from him! If you pass with pain and reluctance, fourth hand will surely pass, thanking you for the warning.

There is practically no hand good enough for a slam when your partner opens with a non-vulnerable three-bid. He probably has only 4 points in high cards, so that you need something like an opening bid of 3 NT (25 to 27 points) in your own hand to feel assured of a slam. Unless you have this sort of powerhouse, you need an extreme freak — something like 7-5-1-0 distribution, with two aces and a 5-card fit with partner's suit!

361. ♠ K 10 9 5 4   ♡ A Q 9 7 6 3 2   ◊ 4   ♣ —

Bid six spades in response to partner's opening bid of three spades, whether vulnerable or not.

You can be a trifle more enterprising when your side is vulnerable. Assume that your partner has something like a seven-card suit headed by K-Q-J. Bid a slam if you can supply everything that is needed.

As we have seen, the opening bid of four in a suit is less common and somewhat stronger. Hence you need less as responder to bid a slam. Give your partner credit for about seven or eight playing tricks, depending on vulnerability, and bid a slam if you can take care of the rest. You need at least two aces, usually three, to consider a slam in this position. Your partner will have no aces in his shutout hand.

It is possible, but not particularly helpful, to make some exploratory bid or other in response to a shutout bid. It is important to remember that you practically never try to get into a better trump suit; you either accept your partner's suit or try to play the hand at notrump (if he will let you do so). Thus, the response in a new suit is forcing:

South	North
3 ♠	4 ♡

South must not pass. Presumably, North is considering a slam in spades.

At any rate, that is what is meant by *experts*. When one or both players are of lesser skill, guesswork must take the place of system. If South is a weak player, North should not make any bid of an exploratory nature; he may be dropped in a cue bid. If North is a weak player, South should beware of assuming that his responses are slam tries; North may simply be looking foolishly for a better trump suit.

When both partners are experts, there is one exception to the rule that responses in a new suit are forcing:

South	North
3 ♡	4 ♠

North expects to play the hand at four spades. If he wished to force, he would have bid only *three* spades. This is, of course, a very rare situation.

One other response may require some attention:

South	North
3 ♡	4 NT

This would be a silly time to use the Blackwood Convention, since South should not have any aces for his three heart bid. Presumably, North's bid should mean: "Bid a slam if you have maximum values for your three-bid. Otherwise, bid only five of your suit."

If North is a bad player, he probably intends his bid to be the Blackwood Convention. South should cautiously bid five clubs in the hope of avoiding disaster. This is usually a forlorn hope, since a shutout leads to trouble when you catch a weak partner with a fairly good hand.

BIDDING AGAINST A SHUTOUT BID

An opponent's shutout bid will often put you up a tree. If the opponents were smart enough to pre-empt more often, you'd be up that tree more of the time. Don't be ashamed of it; the greatest experts can be stumped by a shutout bid.

If you are playing in a good, ethical game, you must get into the habit of making up your mind quickly. You cannot stew unhappily over an opponent's bid and then, finally, pass. This tells your partner that you have values of some kind — information that he is not legally entitled to. A slow pass of this kind forces him to lean over backward and pass any doubtful hand — even if he thinks that your side has a game in view of the values you should have for your slow pass. If he bids a doubtful hand, he has taken advantage of your hesitation, and the opponents are justified in grumbling about this method of conveying information.

Mind you, this isn't easy. You may pass quickly with a hand that is really just barely worth a bid. Or you may hesitate and decide to bid or double with a hand that is not quite worth any action. If you hesitate and then pass on very rare occasions, you will be forgiven by reasonable opponents. If you do this regularly, however, experts will not enjoy playing with or against you. (You may also have a few stormy scenes about this kind of failing.)

Most experts bid a long suit (over the shutout) to show a good trump suit in a hand that is considerably stronger than a minimum opening bid. With a hand that will probably produce a game, they jump right to game in the suit. A bid of three notrump is a natural bid; they expect to play the hand right there. A double is *co-operative*: partner is expected to take out, but he may pass with balanced distribution and some strength in the enemy's suit.

For example:

	South	West	North	East
	3 ♡	?		

362. ♠ K Q J 9 7 5   ♡ 8 4   ◇ A K 9   ♣ 7 2

Bid three spades. You would prefer to have better distribution, particularly fewer losing hearts, but you cannot afford to pass so good a hand.

363. ♠ K J 9 7 6 3   ♡ 8 4   ◇ A K 9   ♣ 7 2

Pass. (And make sure that you pass quickly enough.) The hand has no future unless your partner is strong enough to act by himself. A bid of three spades might put you right in the soup! South has announced a bad hand, but you don't know anything at all about North's hand.

364. ♠ A K Q J 6 3 2   ♡ 4   ◇ A K 9   ♣ 7 2

Bid four spades. You can win nine tricks in your own hand and will make game if partner has as little as the queen of diamonds or the king of clubs.

365. ♠ A J 6 3   ♡ 8   ◇ A K 9 4   ♣ Q J 7 5

Double. If partner has a *very* bad hand, you will be in trouble. You can't afford to hold back, however, since there may be a play for game if he has as little as a couple of kings. The double is for takeout, but partner is allowed to pass for penalties if he has balanced distribution and a trump trick or so. If that is the case, you should beat three hearts.

366. ♠ K J 6 3   ♡ 8 5   ◇ A J 9 4   ♣ Q J 7

Pass. You have no reason to look for a game unless your partner has a better hand than you have. If that is the case, let *him* take the action. If he has a hand of lesser value, you are better off staying out of the auction.

367. ♠ 6 3   ♡ K J 9 8   ◇ A K 9   ♣ Q J 7 2

Pass. If you double, your partner will take out, probably in spades. The best chance for a good result is to pass and hope that your partner will reopen with a double — which you will be delighted to pass for penalties.

368. ♠ K 3   ♡ K J 8   ◇ A Q J 9 4 3   ♣ A 10

Bid three notrump. This sort of bid almost invariably is based on a long suit and scattered strength, including at least one stopper in the enemy's suit.

RESPONDING TO A DOUBLE

When your partner doubles a shutout bid, he expects you to name your best suit. He is aware that you may have a ghastly hand. He may be prepared to drop you like a radioactive potato if you make a minimum response. It therefore follows that you must give him some encouragement when you have any substantial values.

For example:

South	West	North	East
3 ♡	Double	Pass	?

369. ♠ 8 7 6 3   ♡ J 8 4   ◇ K 10 8 3   ♣ 7 2

Bid three spades. You may well be in for trouble, but it would be a mistake to pass.

370. ♠ 8 7 6 3   ♡ K 10 8 3   ◇ J 8 4   ♣ 7 2

Pass. You will probably make two trump tricks, and your partner should take enough side tricks to earn a neat plus.

371. ♠ J 8 7 5 3   ♡ 7 2   ◇ K 10 8 3   ♣ Q 2

Bid three spades. You expect no trouble, but you cannot show real enthusiasm.

372. ♠ Q J 8 6 3   ♡ 7 2   ◇ K 10 8 3   ♣ K 2

Bid four spades. You should have a good play for game opposite any sensible takeout double. If you bid only three spades, your partner may have to pass for fear that you have something like Hand No. 369.

373. ♠ J 8 6 3   ♡ 7   ◇ K 10 8 3   ♣ K Q 7 2

Bid four hearts. This cue bid is forcing to game and asks partner to pick the suit.

THE FISHBEIN CONVENTION

As we have seen, it is often difficult to nail the enemy in a bad spot when they have opened with a bid of three in a weak suit. If you double, your partner takes out; if you pass, your partner may also pass.

For this reason, Harry J. Fishbein, the famous New York expert, devised a method of bidding over shutouts:

a. The double is for penalties (when the shutout bid is at your right, but not if it is passed around to you).

b. The cheapest suit-bid is for takeout and does not promise a biddable holding.

c. Any other bid has its natural meaning.

You have probably heard this convention discussed, and perhaps your partners in rubber bridge have suggested it to you. My advice is to decline the suggestion with thanks.

Unless you are playing in a very expert game, your opponents will seldom make three-bids in horribly weak suits. Hence you will seldom want to double them for penalties; and unless you want to do this, the Fishbein Convention can only lose. Don't forget that you cannot double for a takeout if you are using the Fishbein Convention. You must use the artificial bid in a different suit, and this sometimes causes confusion (particularly if there are some weak players in the game). Moreover, you lose the chance of doubling for a takeout and finding that your partner is delighted to pass for penalties.

My advice, then, is to do without the Fishbein Convention, so far as your own partnership is concerned. If the opponents are using Fishbein, however, don't forget about it. Beef up your own three-bids slightly in order to avoid giving the next player the chance to double for penalties. Avoid the impudent type of three-bid on a suit headed by Q-9, but there is no reason to avoid a suit headed by something like Q-J-10. It still pays to be bold with your shutout bids.

LATER BIDS BY THE OPENER'S SIDE

When your partner has opened with a pre-emptive bid, he has usually told his full story (and sometimes more!) in one bid. Don't put him under severe strain. Don't double the opponents unless you have them set in your own hand. Remember that the distribution is freakish. Your aces will probably take tricks, and so will your trumps; but your kings may be doomed.

Don't double the enemy in one spot unless you are ready to double them in *any other* spot. It would be foolish to warn them away from the one contract you can really beat!

Now for the opening bidder. You have told your story in your opening bid. Don't say anything more unless forced. If your partner doubles, trust him. He should know that you have a worthless hand. If you take the double out, you may well run from a substantial plus to a substantial minus. (If your partner is unreliable, stick with the double anyway; you have a *chance* for a plus score that way, while you are sure to land in the soup if you bid again.)

The cardinal sin is to bid again if your shutout fails to keep the enemy out of the auction. You have done your duty in your opening bid; say nothing more. Consider all the terrible things that can happen if you speak up again:

a. The opponents were in a terrible contract, and your partner was quietly counting the profits until you queered the pitch.

b. The opponents had a cold slam and failed to bid it. Now you give them a second chance.

c. The opponents were undecided whether or not to double you for penalties at three. You have now given them a chance to double you at *four*.

You cannot expect to score a great success with all of your shutout bids. Be satisfied if a portion of them shut the enemy out or push them into a bad contract. If the opponents are lucky enough to bid against you and land on their feet, pass and wait for your next chance to put them to the test.

SHUTOUT BIDS IN THIRD POSITION

After your partner has passed you may open with a shutout bid even if you have slight strength in a side suit (such as an ace or a king). If the hand is otherwise appropriate for a shutout bid you needn't fear missing a slam. If the hand has the strength of a normal opening bid of one in a suit, bid just one. You may miss a game by opening with three of your long suit.

QUIZ No. 29

Neither side is vulnerable, and you are the dealer. What do you say with each of the following hands?

374.	♠ 7 4	♡ K J 9 8 4 3 2	◊ 8 5 3	♣ 4
375.	♠ 7 4	♡ K J 9 8 4 3	◊ Q 8 5 3	♣ 4
376.	♠ 7 4	♡ K J 9 8 4 3	◊ A 8 5 3	♣ 4
377.	♠ 10 7 4 3	♡ Q 8 5	◊ K J 9 8 4 3	♣ —
378.	♠ 5	♡ 10 9 7 6 5 3 2	◊ 8 5 3	♣ J 4
379.	♠ 5	♡ K Q 9 7 6 5 3 2	◊ 8 5 3	♣ 4
380.	♠ 5	♡ A K Q 9 7 5 3	◊ 8 5 3	♣ 4 2

QUIZ No. 30

Both sides are vulnerable, and you are the dealer. What do you say with each of the following hands?

381.	♠ 8 5	♡ K Q 7 6 5 3	◊ J 7 4 2	♣ 4
382.	♠ 8 5	♡ K Q J 7 6 5 3	◊ J 7 4 2	♣ —
383.	♠ 5	♡ K Q J 7 6 5 3	◊ J 8 7 4 2	♣ —
384.	♠ 5	♡ K Q J 10 6 5	◊ K J 8 7	♣ 8 3
385.	♠ 5	♡ 9 2	◊ K Q 10 9 6 5 3	♣ Q J 8

QUIZ No. 31

With both sides vulnerable, the bidding has been:

South	West	North	East
3 ♡	Pass	?	

386. ♠ K Q 9 8 7 5   ♡ 4   ♢ A 9 3   ♣ K 8 5
387. ♠ K Q 9 8 7 5   ♡ A 9 3   ♢ 4   ♣ K 8 5
388. ♠ 8 7 5   ♡ A 9 3 2   ♢ 4 2   ♣ 8 5 3 2
389. ♠ Q J 5 2   ♡ 9 3   ♢ K Q 4 2   ♣ K Q J
390. ♠ A Q 5 2   ♡ 9 3   ♢ K Q 4 2   ♣ K Q J

QUIZ No. 32

With both sides vulnerable, the bidding has been:

South	West	North	East
3 ♡	3 ♠	?	

391. ♠ 5   ♡ K 9 3   ♢ J 8 7 6 2   ♣ K Q 7 4
392. ♠ 5   ♡ A 9 3 2   ♢ 6 2   ♣ K Q J 7 4 3
393. ♠ 10 8 7 6 2   ♡ A 9 3 2   ♢ —   ♣ K Q J 7
394. ♠ K J 10 6 2   ♡ 9 3   ♢ K 6 2   ♣ 7 5 3
395. ♠ A J 10 6   ♡ 3   ♢ K Q 7 2   ♣ Q J 10 8

QUIZ No. 33

With both sides vulnerable, the bidding has been:

South	West	North	East
3 ♡	?		

396. ♠ A Q 8 7 5   ♡ 8   ♢ K Q 9 6   ♣ J 7 4
397. ♠ A Q J 8 7 5   ♡ 8   ♢ K Q 9 6   ♣ 7 4
398. ♠ A Q 8 7 5   ♡ 8   ♢ K Q 9 6   ♣ A K 4
399. ♠ A Q J 10 8 7 5   ♡ 8   ♢ A Q J 6   ♣ 4
400. ♠ 8 7 5   ♡ A J 9 8   ♢ A Q J 6   ♣ K 2
401. ♠ K 5   ♡ A J 9 8   ♢ A Q J 9 6   ♣ K 2
402. ♠ K 5   ♡ K 9   ♢ A K Q J 9 6 3   ♣ A 4

QUIZ No. 34

With both sides vulnerable, the bidding has been:

South	West	North	East
3 ◇	Double	Pass	?

403. ♠ 8 5 4   ♡ J 9 6 3 2   ◇ 8 5   ♣ 9 6 2
404. ♠ 5 4   ♡ J 9 6 3   ◇ J 10 8 5   ♣ K J 2
405. ♠ 5 4   ♡ K Q 9 6 3   ◇ 8 5   ♣ K J 6 2
406. ♠ K J 6 2   ♡ K Q 9 6 3   ◇ 8 5   ♣ 5 4
407. ♠ K J 6 2   ♡ K Q 9 6 3   ◇ —   ♣ A 9 6 2

7. Slam Bidding

Nobody bids all of the makable slams. Nobody stays out of all the unmakable slams. The best players in the world have a rather spotty record in slam bidding.

There is a natural and logical reason for this. It is reasonable to bid a slam when you have an even chance — say a finesse — to make it. Slams of this kind are defeated just as often as they are made. Hence you may bid perfectly reasonable slams and still be defeated.

Even though *perfection* is out of reach, *improvement* in your slam bidding is always possible. The fastest way to improve is to study the auctions that most commonly lead to slams.

AFTER A DOUBLE RAISE

It is always advisable to think about a slam when your partner has raised your suit from one to three. Thus:

South	North
1 ♡	3 ♡
?	

North shows strong support for hearts in a hand counting 13 to 17 points. South should begin to think about a slam if he has 15 or 16 points. The combined total may then be close to the 33 points usually needed for slam.

For example:

408. ♠ 8 3   ♡ A Q 8 6 3   ◇ K J 5   ♣ A K 3

South has 17 points in high cards and may count extra points for the fifth heart and for the doubleton in spades. The combined hands may or may not produce a slam. South should tertainly *think* about a slam and should look for a way to find out what he wants to know.

409. ♠ 8 3   ♡ A Q 8 6 3   ◊ K J 5   ♣ A 3 2

South has only 14 points in high cards. Even if he counts extra points for his distribution, he should not think seriously about a slam. The reason is that South has a minimum opening bid. If you changed the king of diamonds to a low card, South would be very reluctant to open the bidding. Even if you changed the queen of hearts to a low card, South would have a very doubtful opening bid. You could remove the jack of diamonds, but that's about all. A hand that is only a jack better than a minimum opening bid should not make the first move towards a slam in this situation.

What does South need, as a minimum, to think about slam? With balanced distribution, he should have an ace better than a minimum opening bid. With unbalanced distribution (singleton or void suit), he should have a king better than a minimum opening bid.

Mind you, possession of the extra ace or king doesn't entitle you to bid the slam. It merely entitles you to make a *slam try*.

Which bids are slam tries in this situation? Any bid in a new suit, such as three spades, four clubs, or four diamonds. A jump to five hearts would likewise be a slam try. A bid of four notrump would be a special kind of slam try — the Blackwood Convention.

A jump to five notrump would be a slam demand rather than a slam try. North would be expected to choose between six hearts and six notrump.

A bid of three notrump or four hearts would indicate that South was not at all interested in a slam. North would be expected to pass four hearts, but might take three notrump out to four of the major.

Which type of slam try should South make? The answer depends on the nature of South's hand, and whether he is more anxious to give, or to receive information. South picks the kind of slam try that best describes his hand or that is most likely to produce the information that he needs for a sensible decision.

THE BLACKWOOD CONVENTION

The Blackwood Convention is a useful weapon, but most players overuse it. They ask partner how many aces he holds and then don't know what to do when they get the answer. (Note that a repeat Blackwood bid of 5 NT asking for kings guarantees that the partnership holds all four aces.) Many players act as though it is illegal, or perhaps shameful, to bid a slam without first saying the magic words *four notrump*. Most experts use the Blackwood Convention on only one slam hand out of four or five.

The time to use the Convention is when you are considering a *grand* slam or when your suits are headed by king-queen combinations, with no dangerous weak doubleton.

For example, after a double raise from one to three hearts:

410. ♠ 8   ♡ A K J 6 2   ◇ K Q J 9 4   ♣ K 3

Bid four notrump. If partner shows three aces, you will bid a grand slam. If he shows two aces, you will stop at six hearts. If he shows only one ace, you will stop at *five* hearts. An ideal hand for the Blackwood Convention because you have all the *second-round controls*—kings or singletons. You need to know only about first-round controls—aces.

411. ♠ Q 7   ♡ A K J 6 2   ◇ K Q 9 4   ♣ K 3

Bid four diamonds, *not* four notrump. Your partner will get you to a slam if he has three aces; and he will discourage you from bidding a slam if he has only one ace. No special convention is needed for these cases. The problem arises when he has *two* aces. If you discover this fact, as you can by means of the Black-wood Convention, you still won't know what to do. You may have two losing spades; perhaps not. The point is that guesswork will take the place of skill. The bid of four diamonds (or four clubs) gives you the chance to find out what you want to know. A psychic bid of three spades may discourage a spade lead and thus permit you to make an "unmakable" slam. We shall discuss all of these possibilities later. At this moment our point is that the Blackwood Convention is *not* the right weapon for this hand.

Before we leave this brief discussion of Blackwood, let's consider which bids of four notrump are conventional and which are not.

In the average game, almost any bid of four notrump may be treated as conventional. Your good sense may tell you that certain bids of four notrump have only their natural meaning, but your partner may not have the same good sense — or he may be in doubt about *your* good sense.

From this we derive our first rule for average games: Don't bid four notrump unless you are willing to have your partner treat it as a Blackwood bid. Our second rule is similar: Don't pass a strange partner in four notrump; he may believe he is making a Blackwood bid.

You don't have to follow these rules when you are playing with a familiar and reliable partner. These notrump raises are not Blackwood:

South	North
1 NT	4 NT (not Blackwood)

South	North
2 NT	4 NT (not Blackwood)

A raise to four notrump where no suit has been bid is clearly just a natural bid, and not at all conventional.

When only one suit bid has been made, it is possible to play the bid of four notrump either way:

South	North
1 ♠	2 NT
4 NT	

Some experts prefer to treat this as a raise in notrump,

asking partner to go on if he has close to 15 points, but to stop short if he has close to 13 points for his jump to 2 NT. Other experts prefer to treat this as the Blackwood Convention.

When the one suit has been bid and raised, a bid of four notrump is clearly Blackwood:

South	North
1 NT	3 ♡
4 ♡	4 NT

CUE BIDS

A cue bid is a bid in a suit that the player clearly doesn't seriously suggest as a trump suit; for example a suit bid by an opponent. In most situations the cue bid is meant as a slam try. In a few cases, at the lower levels, a player may make a cue bid to show a stopper or to ask for help in stopping a suit for notrump purposes. If the cue bid is made beyond three notrump or if the cue-bidder himself goes beyond three notrump later, it is clear that he had a slam in mind.

A cue bid usually shows an ace or a void but may instead show some general slam interest or may be made in the hope of deceiving the enemy. In Hand No. 408, for example, South should make the cue bid of four clubs. With Hand No. 411, South should bid four diamonds if he wants to make an "honest" cue bid. As we have noted, he may instead bid three spades in the hope of talking the opening leader out of a spade lead.

While we are on the subject of fake cue bids, let's neither over-rate nor under-rate them. They have much the same importance as bluffs in poker. A player who never bluffs is easy to read. It is advisable to make an occasional fake cue bid to keep your opponents on the anxious seat. You will get occasional unexpected benefits when a suspicious opponent leads a suit that you have bid quite honestly.

It isn't important for the cue bid to mean anything very definite. What is important is that the responder has the chance to show values if he is interested in a slam and to sign off in the agreed suit if he has already overbid or if the hand just doesn't look slamworthy. For example:

South	North
1 ♡	3 ♡
4 ♣	4 ♡
4 ♠	6 ♡

In this sequence, South's bid of four clubs is a cue bid, suggesting a slam and promising strength in clubs, probably the ace. North signs off by bidding four hearts.

Undiscouraged, South tries again with a cue bid in spades. This shows that his hand is strong enough to guarantee a contract of five hearts. His bid promises strength in spades.

What does South need for the slam that he is so obviously trying to reach? He must be worried about diamonds; perhaps also about the solidity of the hearts. His message is: "Partner, I already know that you have minimum values for your double raise. Nevertheless, I am still interested in a slam. Can you give me the right sort of help in the red suits?"

South might have such a hand as:

412. ♠ A 5   ♡ A J 9 8 5   ◊ J 6   ♣ A K J 3

North would first sign off and later bid the slam with:

413. ♠ K 3   ♡ K Q 7 6 4   ◊ K Q 8 5   ♣ 9 2

But North would sign off again at five hearts with:

414. ♠ K Q 3   ♡ K Q 10 7 6   ◊ Q 10 8 5   ♣ 9

A player isn't always strong enough to make *two* cue bids. In the case of Hand No. 408, for example, South can make a try for the slam by bidding four clubs. If North signs off at four hearts, South must yield gracefully and play the hand at that contract.

Even if North responds with a bid of four diamonds, showing the ace of that suit, South can bid only four hearts. He has made a slam try, but he cannot drive the bidding past game. If North makes a further try by bidding four spades — the suit that South is really worried about — South will accept the invitation and go right to six hearts.

SLAM BIDDING AFTER A JUMP TAKEOUT

The jump takeout announces that slam is possible even if the opening bidder has a minimum. For example:

South	North
1 ♡	2 ♠

South should immediately consider the value of his hand for a slam. He can begin the process of signing off by making a minimum rebid in notrump or by rebidding his suit. In rare cases, the opener may rebid in a new suit without getting too high; but this usually encourages the responder to look for a slam.

Good distribution or a fit for the responder's suit may be enough to sway the opening bidder towards a slam. He encourages a slam by raising his partner, by making any jump rebid (seldom necessary), or by bidding a new suit — especially if he subsequently shows any sign of life.

For example, with the bidding given above:

415. ♠ 8 7 4   ♡ A K J 9 4   ◇ K Q 2   ♣ 9 3

Bid three hearts. Begin signing off. Partner will have to tug and haul before you show much interest in slam.

416. ♠ 8 7 4   ♡ A K J 9 4   ◇ A Q 2   ♣ 9 3

Bid three hearts. You will try for a slam if partner shows a good heart fit. The difference between a side ace and a side king is tremendous when you are thinking about slam.

417. ♠ K 7 4   ♡ A K J 9 4   ◇ Q J 2   ♣ 9 3

Bid three spades. The fit for partner's suit may be the key to a successful slam.

418. ♠ 7 4   ♡ A K J 9   ◇ K Q 6 2   ♣ J 9 3

Bid two notrump. No fit for spades, no rebiddable suit, no new suit to show, minimum strength.

419. ♠ 7 4   ♡ A K Q J 9 4   ◇ K Q 2   ♣ 9 3

Bid four hearts. This sort of jump guarantees a solid suit. You are willing to play for slam in hearts opposite a singleton.

420. ♠ J 4   ♡ A K J 9   ◇ A Q 6 2   ♣ Q 9 3

Bid three notrump. Balanced distribution, strength in the unbid suits, and about 16 to 18 points in high cards. The partnership will not stop short of slam.

The responder should have few problems at his second turn. When he made his jump takeout, he promised either a very strong suit of his own; fine support for partner's suit; or tremendous high-card strength. With the independent suit, he rebids that suit; with support, he raises partner; with tremendous strength, he can usually bid notrump.

South	North
1 ♡	2 ♠
3 ♡	?

421. ♠ A K Q J 7 5 2   ♡ 8 3   ◇ 8   ♣ A K 10 2

Bid three spades. You will later use the Blackwood Convention on your way to at least six spades.

422. ♠ A Q J 7   ♡ Q 10 8 3   ◇ 8 4   ♣ A K 10

Bid four hearts. Partner is expected to move towards a slam unless he has the worst of minimum opening bids.

423. ♠ A Q J 7 5   ♡ Q 10 8 3   ◇ 8   ♣ A K 10

Bid four clubs. You will bid at least five hearts at your next turn, thus showing your fine support and your singleton in the unbid suit at the same time. (A player who bids three suits as strongly as this guarantees a singleton or void in the fourth suit.)

424. ♠ A Q J 7 5   ♡ 8 3   ◊ A 4   ♣ A K 10 2

Bid three notrump. This kind of rebid indicates that you have at least 18 points in high cards, with neither a tremendous suit of your own nor good support for partner's suit. Partner is expected to bid again if he can visualize slam opposite this promised strength.

SLAM BIDDING WITH SINGLETONS

It's usually fairly easy to bid a slam when the combined strength counts to about 33 points in high cards, particularly when a long suit is available or when a suit has been bid and raised. The slam can often be made with about 29 points, or even less, when one member of the partnership has a singleton in the right suit.

For example, consider the following partnership hands:

425.

West	East
♠ K 7	♠ A 8 2
♡ A Q J 7 5	♡ K 10 6 3
◊ 5 3 2	◊ 6
♣ A 9 4	♣ K Q J 7 4

The combined hands are virtually sure to make a slam in either hearts or clubs, but the high-card strength is only 27 points!

How do the partners reach this laydown slam?

The answer is simple in this case, but it must be admitted that slams based on "fit" are the most difficult to bid. It is necessary for both partners to bid informatively and for each to visualize the value his hand has.

In this case, the bidding would be:

West	East
1 ♡	2 ♣
2 ♡	2 ♠
3 ♣	4 ♡
6 ♡	Pass

East bids the clubs, makes a "reverse" bid in spades, and then makes a jump raise in hearts. The effect is to show strength in the bid suits and a singleton in the unbid diamonds. West can see the slam very easily and should therefore bid it.

Change the West hand slightly:

426. ♠ 5 3 2   ♡ A Q J 7 5   ◇ K 7   ♣ A 9 4

The diamonds and spades have been exchanged, but the hand is otherwise the same. West stops at four hearts, and doesn't even consider bidding a slam. His king of diamonds opposite the announced singleton is obvious *duplication of values*. This hand might produce twelve tricks with reasonable suit breaks, but West cannot try for it with a minimum opening bid and duplication. The case would be even worse if the hand were changed more:

427. ♠ 5 3 2   ♡ A Q J 7 5   ◇ A K 7   ♣ 9 4

The ace-king of diamonds are opposite the announced singleton, and now a spade opening lead will surely defeat a slam contract. The opening bidder should stop at game.

The device of showing a singleton can be used likewise by the opening bidder:

South	North
1 ♡	1 ♠
3 ♣	3 NT
4 ♠	

It is clear that South was ready to support spades at the time he bid clubs. Hence the jump in clubs and the delayed spade raise are part of a *bidding sequence*. South thus shows a very strong hand with a singleton in the unbid suit. For example:

428. ♠ K Q 4 3   ♡ A Q J 6 3   ◇ 4   ♣ A Q 5

North should go on if he can visualize a slam opposite a hand of this nature. This will especially be true if he has a moderately good hand with three small diamonds or so. It will still be true if he has one of the missing aces and both of the fitting kings (hearts and clubs). For example:

429. ♠ J 10 9 7 5   ♡ K 9   ◊ A 7 3   ♣ K 8 4

North should confidently move towards slam in spades. He knows that his partner has a singleton diamond, fine support for spades, and fine values in hearts and clubs. What more is needed?

It is important to notice that in both of the previous bidding sequences it was possible to suggest a slam without going past game. The player who had a singleton was able to show it and could then await his partner's decision. If the singleton happened to fit well, partner would bid slam; otherwise, he would be safe at game.

Another important item to notice is that the eventual show of trump support must come in such a way that it is obviously strong support rather than grudging support. The following sequence is far from clear:

South	North
1 ♡	1 ♠
3 ♣	3 ♠
4 ♠	

South doesn't guarantee fine spades and a singleton diamond in this case. He may have two very good suits of his own and may have raised spades because North was unable to support either hearts or clubs.

A clearer auction is:

South	North
1 ♡	1 ♠
3 ♣	3 ♡
3 ♠	

The support for spades is voluntary rather than grudging. When the support is shown in a *jump* raise, the indications are that *considerable* trump strength is held:

	South		North
	1 ♡		1 ♠
	3 ♣		3 ♡
	4 ♠		

South should have four spades headed by at least Q-J, probably better. The hearts must be at least five cards in length, and South must have a singleton diamond. Since the club bid does not show a real suit, it must be a cue bid, showing the ace. In short, South shows a hand of this nature:

430.　♠ K Q 7 4　　♡ A K J 9 3　　◊ 6　　♣ A J 2

SLAM BIDDING AFTER AN OPENING TWO-BID

The opening two-bid has not been treated separately in this book because it isn't much of a problem for the experienced player. There is, however, some problem about sorting out the game from the slam hands after an opening two-bid.

The opening two-bid promises a very reasonable play for game opposite almost any nondescript hand. It should also promise either exceptionally freakish distribution, or strength in three suits. An experienced player should use his judgment and a few general rules rather than try to apply any arithmetical formula.

For example:

430.　♠ A K Q 8 5　　♡ A K Q 7 4　　◊ 5 3　　♣ 6

Most experts will avoid opening this hand with *two* spades, even though game at spades or hearts is a very good gamble. Add a spade or a heart, making the distribution more freakish, and they will take the plunge.

431.　♠ A K J 8 5　　♡ A K Q 7 4　　◊ A 3　　♣ 6

Most experts will open this hand with two spades even though it is not necessarily stronger in playing strength than Hand No. 430. The difference is that this hand has strength in *three* suits rather than only two suits.

The reason for the insistence on strength in three suits is that the responder may get you too high if you open a *two*-suiter with a two-bid. This, in turn, depends on the very sound principle that the responder (the *weaker* of the two partnership hands) must display most of the enterprise and initiative in bidding towards a slam after a two-bid.

Let's see the reason for that. The requirements for an opening bid of two in a suit are so high that you seldom have much *extra* strength after you have made this opening bid. You may use your second or third bid to finish the picture of your distribution, but you seldom have much to say about your strength that you didn't say in your opening bid.

The situation can be compared to the opening bid of one notrump. The responder knows that the opening bidder has 16 to 18 points with balanced distribution and at least three suits stopped. The opening bidder knows nothing (to start with) about his partner's hand. The player who *knows* must take the initiative rather than the player who doesn't know.

Much the same is true after the opening bid of two in a suit. The responder knows a great deal about the opening hand; the opener knows very little about the responding hand. Hence the responder must usually decide whether to try for a slam or to be content with a mere game.

The responder will show enterprise whenever he has a fit for the opening bidder's main suit together with some *useful* high card on the side. Since most two-bids include a singleton or void suit (a *balanced* strong hand would be opened with two or three *notrump* rather than two of a suit), the responder doesn't get excited over an ace or king-queen combination in a side suit; it may duplicate the opening bidder's short suit. But if the responder has strength of this kind in *two* suits, he is justified in believing that one suit or the other will be useful. It is up to him to show signs of ambition, and he will do so.

This kind of ambition will be safe enough if the opening

bidder has strength in three suits. It will be dangerous if the opener has strength in only two suits.

Now let's see how the responder shows his enterprise. He should be on the lookout to show 7 points or more in high card strength by means of a *positive* response. The negative response is two notrump; any other response is positive. For example:

South	North
2 ♡	?

432. ♠ K J 8 5 4   ♡ 6 2   ◇ K 8 5   ♣ 7 3 2
Bid two spades. The bare minimum for a positive response.

433. ♠ 7 3 2   ♡ 6 2   ◇ K 8 5   ♣ K J 8 5 4
Bid two notrump. Avoid increasing the bidding level with minimum values and no fit.

434. ♠ 7 3 2   ♡ K 8 5   ◇ 6 2   ♣ K J 8 5 4
Bid three hearts. You are happy to show the fit, despite the minimum values.

435. ♠ Q 3 2   ♡ 6 2   ◇ K 8 5   ♣ K J 8 5 4
Bid three notrump. The jump distinguishes your bid from the negative response of only *two* notrump.

436. ♠ K 3 2   ♡ 6 2   ◇ K 8 5   ♣ K Q 8 5 4
Bid three clubs. The jump to three notrump shows about 9 or 10 points. With 11 points or more in good combinations, you should plan to make at least two bids. Show your long suit first and make an unmistakable slam try at your next turn.

437. ♠ K 3 2   ♡ K 8 5   ◇ 6 2   ♣ K Q 8 5 4
Bid three clubs. You intend to reach at least five hearts, but there is no harm in showing your long suit first.

438. ♠ A 3 2   ♡ K 8 5   ◇ 6 2   ♣ K Q 8 5 4
Bid three clubs. You will not stop short of *six* hearts. First,

however, you show your long suit. If partner has the ace of clubs, he may rely on your long suit to make a try for a *grand* slam.

Incidentally, Hand No. 438 illustrates the principle of showing suits rather than aces in response to an opening two-bid. A few experts advocate showing aces immediately in response to two-bids, but they are in a clear minority (in quality as well as quantity). Anybody can make up a few sample hands to argue on either side of this question, but the experience of most of the great players supports the principle of responding with distribution rather than with aces.

QUIZ No. 35

	South	North
	1 ♠	3 ♠
	?	

439.	♠ A J 8 7 2	♡ A K 4	◇ 9 6 2	♣ 8 5
440.	♠ A J 8 7 2	♡ A K 8 4	◇ 9 6 2	♣ 5
441.	♠ A J 8 7 2	♡ A K 8 4	◇ K 6 2	♣ 5
442.	♠ A J 8 7 2	♡ A K 4	◇ A 6 2	♣ 8 5
443.	♠ A J 8 7 2	♡ A K 4	◇ K Q 2	♣ 8 5
444.	♠ A J 8 7 2	♡ A K 8 7 2	◇ 6 2	♣ 5
445.	♠ A J 8 7 2	♡ A K 8 7 2	◇ K 2	♣ 5
446.	♠ A Q 8 7 2	♡ A K Q 7 2	◇ K 2	♣ 5
447.	♠ A K J 7 2	♡ K Q J 7 2	◇ K 2	♣ 5
448.	♠ A K J 7 2	♡ K Q J 7 2	◇ A 5 2	♣ —

QUIZ No. 36

	South	North
	1 ♠	3 ♠
	4 ◇	?

449.	♠ Q 10 6 3	♡ 9 5 3	◇ K Q 8 4	♣ K Q
450.	♠ Q 10 6 3	♡ A 5 3	◇ J 9 8 4	♣ K Q
451.	♠ Q 10 6 3	♡ A 5 3	◇ Q J 8 4	♣ K Q

452.	♠ Q 10 6 3	♡ K Q 9 5 3	◇ 8 4	♣ K Q
453.	♠ K J 6 3	♡ K Q 9 3	◇ K Q 8 4	♣ 5
454.	♠ K 8 6 3	♡ K Q 9 3	◇ K 8 4	♣ A 5
455.	♠ K J 6 3 2	♡ A 3	◇ K Q 8 7 4	♣ 5
456.	♠ K J 6 3 2	♡ K 3	◇ K Q J 8 7 4	♣ —

QUIZ No. 37

South	North
1 ♠	3 ♠
4 ◇	4 ♡
?	

457.	♠ A Q J 8 3	♡ 9 6 2	◇ A K 3	♣ Q 8
458.	♠ A Q J 8 3	♡ K 6 2	◇ A K 3	♣ Q 8
459.	♠ A Q J 8 3	♡ Q 6 2	◇ A K Q 7 3	♣ —
460.	♠ A J 8 7 3	♡ —	◇ A K J 7 3	♣ Q J 4
461.	♠ A J 8 7 3	♡ Q J 4	◇ A K J 7 3	♣ —

QUIZ No. 38

South	North
1 ♡	3 ♣
?	

462.	♠ 6 3 2	♡ A Q J 9 4	◇ K Q J 8 5	♣ —
463.	♠ —	♡ A Q J 9 4	◇ K Q J 8 5	♣ 6 3 2
464.	♠ —	♡ A Q J 9 4	◇ A K J 8 5	♣ 6 3 2
465.	♠ K 4	♡ A Q J 9	◇ K J 8 5	♣ 6 3 2
466.	♠ 6 3 2	♡ A Q J 9	◇ K J 8 5	♣ K 4
467.	♠ 6 3 2	♡ A Q J 9	◇ A J 8 5	♣ K 4
468.	♠ 6 2	♡ A Q J 9	◇ K Q 8 5	♣ A 8 4
469.	♠ 6 2	♡ A K J 9 6 3	◇ K Q 8 5	♣ 4
470.	♠ 6 2	♡ A K Q J 6 3	◇ K Q 8 5	♣ 4
471.	♠ A 2	♡ A K Q J 6 3	◇ K Q 8 5	♣ 4

QUIZ No. 39

	South	North
	1 ♡	1 ♠
	?	

	♠	♡	♦	♣
472.	K J 9 4	A K J 7 3	A J 5	8
473.	K J 9 4	A K J 7 3	A J	8 5
474.	K Q 9 4	A K Q 7 3	A Q 5	8
475.	K Q 9 4	A K Q 7 3 2	A J 5	—

QUIZ No. 40

	South	North
	1 ♡	1 ♠
	3 ♣	3 ♡
	4 ♠	?

	♠	♡	♦	♣
476.	A 9 7 3 2	Q 7 4	8 3 2	K 5
477.	J 9 7 3 2	J 7 4	A Q J	Q 5
478.	J 9 7 3 2	K 7 4	A K 2	Q 5
479.	Q J 7 3 2	K Q 4	A 3 2	K 5

8. Defensive Bidding

When an opponent has opened the bidding, you will seldom have a game and will practically never have a slam. The hand usually "belongs" to the opponents.

There is much to be said for staying out of the auction unless there is a *good* reason for coming in. For one thing, if you stay out, you can't be doubled. For another, if you maintain silence, the eventual declarer will have no clue to the location of high cards or suit lengths, and he may flounder instead of proceeding with assurance.

There is also much to be said for entering the auction. For one thing, your side may have a game, or perhaps a part score. For another, you may be able to indicate a favorable opening lead or a good line of defense.

Which view should prevail? The answer depends on many factors: the playing strength of your hand, the vulnerability and part score situation, the level at which you must bid (if you do), the solidity of your suit, your length in the opponent's suit, the bidding habits of the enemy, the relative skill of your partner and the enemy, and even the frame of mind of the various players at the table.

Bidding Habits: You avoid making a doubtful overcall against opponents who double at the drop of a trick. Likewise, you avoid making a doubtful defensive bid of any kind when your partner is a determined overbidder. You tend to make trap passes when the opponents bid loosely and wildly. You tend to overcall when the opponents are conservative bidders and reluctant doublers.

Relative Skill: You avoid sacrifice bid situations when you have a weak partner against strong opponents. In this situation you are not eager to lose a big rubber; take your small licking, and get it over with. Contrariwise, you foster such sacrifice situations when you clearly have the better partnership. It isn't necessary to make dangerous lead-indicating bids when your partner is skillful at picking a "blind" opening lead; but you must take a few risks if your partner is given to wooden and disastrous opening leads.

Frame of Mind: If the opponents have suffered some reverses and are downhearted, you can usually get away with a doubtful bid. Towards the end of a session, if the opponents are eager to win the rubber and call it a day, you can get away with a weak overcall; they will prefer to bid on, instead of doubling you. There are many other emotions and frames of mind, and all may have their effect on what you can safely risk.

GAIN VERSUS LOSS

Most of the other factors have to do with possible gain as against possible loss. If you enter the auction against an opponent's opening bid, you usually stand to gain only a part score — as against letting *them* make a part score. The difference is worth about 300 points. (Nobody knows the true value of a part score at rubber bridge, but it is probably much closer to 100 points than the average player supposes. Hence the difference between winning a part score and letting the opponents make one is about 200 points aside from the difference in the trick scores.)

You can well afford to make an overcall, get doubled, and go down one trick whether vulnerable or not. The loss of 100 or 200 points is usually balanced by the fact that the opponents would make a part score of some kind if you hadn't bid.

Sometimes the opponents must give up a game in order to penalize you. This will often be true if the tricks they take against you consist of aces and kings. It will not be true if the opponents take low-card tricks against you, particularly tricks in your trump suit. The difference is that they can use aces and kings for making a game of their own; but they cannot use low-card tricks, particularly low cards in your trump suit.

It follows that you should make defensive bids only when your suit is fairly solid. For example, you don't mind overcalling with such a hand as:

480. ♠ 8 2   ♡ Q J 10 8 6 3   ◊ K Q J 9   ♣ 3

You expect to lose tricks to the four aces and to the kings of spades and hearts You don't expect to lose any tricks to *low* cards.

You should not dream of overcalling with *this* hand:

481. ♠ 8 3 2   ♡ A Q 6 3 2   ◊ A Q 5   ♣ 9 4

You might well open the bidding with this hand, but you would not make the very same bid — one heart — if an opponent opened the bidding with one club at your right.

Once you have drummed into your subconscious the fact that you cannot afford to overcall on broken suits (this book is not primarily addressed to millionaires), you will automatically reject all the absolutely ghastly and impossible overcalls that make steady losers of most bridge players. Your chief task, then, will be to decide when a hand of the right sort is *worth* an overcall. Here again your yardstick is the Rule of 500 Points (see Chapter 6): If you have a suit of the right sort, you can afford to risk a penalty of 500 points. If the enemy can beat you by that amount *by taking aces and kings,* they should be cold for a game in some spot of their own choosing.

When your hand is worth any action at all, you must decide which bid best describes your hand. You may choose a *simple* overcall in a suit, a *jump* overcall in a suit, an overcall in notrump, a takeout double, or a cue bid in the enemy's suit.

THE SIMPLE OVERCALL

The simple overcall in a suit shows a good suit, safe against a disastrous penalty double. It has limits in high-card strength as well as in playing strength.

The weakest hand that is worth a simple overcall is one that contains the equivalent of K-Q-J in some suit. If your hand contains no king and no ace, either pass it or take some preemptive action with it. Your partner should be able to assume that your hand will probably take at least one defensive trick when you make an overcall.

At the upper range are the hands that, with some help from your partner, will make a game. However, if you can make a game with only a couple of kings in your partner's hand, or perhaps an ace and some other useful card, you should take stronger action than a simple overcall. (As we will soon see, the recommended action is a takeout double, followed by a bid in your good suit.)

For example, assume that neither side is vulnerable, and that the player at your right deals and bids one heart:

482. ♠ K Q J 9 6   ♡ 8 4   ◇ 7 3 2   ♣ 8 5 4

Pass. There is nothing terribly unsound about a bid of one spade, since the hand is probably good for four spade tricks and is thus safe (non-vulnerable) against a disastrous double. The trouble is that this overcall is somewhat pointless. Even if you strike your partner with a good hand, you have no future; in fact, he will probably get you too high.

483. ♠ K Q J 9 6 2   ♡ 8 4   ◇ 7 3   ♣ A 5 4

Bid one spade. The additions of the sixth spade and the side ace make the bid safer and give you some hope of landing on your feet if you strike your partner with a good hand.

484. ♠ Q J 10 9 8 6 2   ♡ 8 4   ◇ 7 3   ♣ 5 4

Do not bid one spade; either pass or take pre-emptive action. (A jump to *two* spades is recommended, as we will soon see.)

485. ♠ 8 5 4   ♡ 8 4   ◊ 7 3   ♣ K Q J 9 6 2

Pass. It is pointless to bid with a hopeless minimum. An overcall at the level of two should suggest some hope that the hand belongs to your side.

486. ♠ K 5 4   ♡ 8 4   ◊ 7 3   ♣ K Q J 9 6 2

Bid two clubs. You will probably win five clubs and a spade, so the bid is reasonably safe. The addition of the king of spades has strengthened the hand enough to justify a bid at the level of two.

487. ♠ K Q J 9 6 2   ♡ 8 4   ◊ A 3   ♣ A J 4

Do not bid one spade; take stronger action. (Double first, and bid the spades later.) You will probably have a play for game if partner has a couple of kings or so.

Since your overcall must be safe against disaster, you need one more trick for a vulnerable than for a non-vulnerable bid. Likewise, you need one more trick for an overcall at the level of two than at the level of one.

RESPONDING TO A SIMPLE OVERCALL

When your partner has made a simple overcall, you know the limits of his hand. He has a good suit, he has enough playing strength to be safe within the limits of the Rule of 500 Points, and he needs more than a couple of kings from your hand to have a reasonable play for game.

If you have only a couple of kings, or less, you can afford to pass. No game will be missed. Exceptionally, you may bid with a weak hand of this sort if you have a good distributional fit for your partner — four or more trumps and shortness in another suit. The idea is to make the bidding difficult for the enemy or to take a sacrifice against their game or part score.

There is little advantage in bidding your own suit with a bad hand unless partner has been doubled for penalties; don't cry before you're hurt. Even then, you *rescue* only when you have good reason to believe that your suit is longer and stronger than your partner's.

When your partner has overcalled at the level of one, you need more than the value of a normal opening bid to think seriously of game. When he has overcalled at the level of two, particularly vulnerable, you need somewhat less than the value of an opening bid to think seriously of game.

When you do have a good hand, think first of raising a major suit or of taking partner from a minor into a good major suit of your own. Think next of notrump possibilities, for which you need at least one sure stopper in the enemy's suit.

Avoid the mistake of bidding your own suit when you can afford to raise your partner's major suit. Since partner's overcall promises a strong suit of five or more cards, you can afford to raise with only three trumps. If you fail to raise, your partner will assume that you are *denying* his suit; and he will tend to pass.

South	West	North	East
1 ♡	1 ♤	Pass	?

488. ♤ 8 5 4   ♡ 9 6   ♢ A J 4 3   ♧ K 9 3 2

Pass. There is no game in this hand. Let sleeping dogs lie.

489. ♤ 9 8 5 4   ♡ 6   ♢ A J 4 3   ♧ K 9 3 2

Bid two spades. Game is very unlikely, but barely possible if partner has a maximum hand for his overcall and some low hearts to be ruffed. In any case, it will do no harm to push the bidding up to the level of two.

490. ♤ 9 8 5 4 3   ♡ 6   ♢ 4 3   ♧ K Q J 3 2

Bid four spades. If this goes down, as is likely, you have the consolation of knowing that the opponents almost surely had a cold game or slam. You are always willing to push the bidding high without delay when you have an excellent fit for partner's suit and very little defensive strength.

491. ♠ 9 8 5 4   ♡ 6   ◇ A J 4 3   ♣ K Q 3 2

Bid two spades. You are seriously interested in game. If partner makes any further bid, you will make sure of getting to game.

492. ♠ 9 8 5 4   ♡ 6   ◇ A K 4 3   ♣ K Q 3 2

Bid three spades. This raise is, of course, a serious try for game. Partner is expected to go on except with the most doubtful of overcalls.

493. ♠ 9 8 5 4   ♡ K 6 2   ◇ A K 3   ♣ K 3 2

Bid two spades. The king of hearts is probably worthless, and the distribution is poor. You must make some sort of gesture towards game, but you can't afford more than this.

494. ♠ 8 5 4   ♡ 6   ◇ A K J 4 3   ♣ K 8 3 2

Bid two spades. Don't bid the diamonds when you can support your partner's major suit. Game is possible, and you will bid it if partner shows a sign of life.

495. ♠ Q 5 4   ♡ 6   ◇ A K J 4 3   ♣ K 8 3 2

Bid three spades. The trump support is ample when your partner has made an overcall. There should be a reasonable play for game unless your partner has the barest minimum overcall.

496. ♠ 6   ♡ 9 3 2   ◇ K Q 9 7 4 2   ♣ 8 3 2

Pass. Don't think about a rescue until you're in trouble. Time enough to consider a bid of two diamonds if your partner is doubled for penalties.

497. ♠ 6   ♡ 9 3   ◇ Q J 10 9 7 4 2   ♣ A 3 2

Pass or two diamonds. If you bid two diamonds now you may have to bid more diamonds later to keep out of spades. It is wiser to pass and bid diamonds as a rescue only if trouble develops.

498. ♠ Q 6   ♡ K J 3   ◇ Q J 10 9   ♣ A J 3 2

Bid one notrump. This type of bid is a serious suggestion of game. Partner is expected to pass or bid two spades with a weak hand; to bid three spades or raise notrump with a good hand.

499. ♠ Q 6   ♡ K J 3   ◇ K J 10 9   ♣ A Q 9 2

Bid two notrump. You intend to reach a game, whether your partner likes it or not. His only chance to stay below game is to pass at two notrump, which he should do with a balanced minimum overcall.

THE JUMP OVERCALL

Some experts use the jump overcall to show a strong hand but most experts prefer to use it for pre-emptive purposes. It will be treated as a pre-emptive bid in this book. The reader is warned to make sure that his partner so understands it. Otherwise, when your partner makes a jump overcall in the average game of rubber bridge, he is probably trying to show you a good hand. This is a subject you would do well to clarify among the players that you regularly play with.

The pre-emptive jump overcall is made on a long suit of reasonable strength, with little or no side strength. The idea is to show a hand of good offensive strength but no defensive strength.

You cannot hope to shut out good opponents when the hand belongs to them. You may make matters difficult for them by robbing them of a level or two of bidding. You may indicate a sound enough suit for your partner to undertake a paying sacrifice. If neither of these benefits happens to materialize, your bid has not paid off, but it hasn't cost you anything either.

As already indicated, a jump overcall is recommended on

Hand No. 484. I would also jump to two spades on Hand No. 483 if it lacked the ace of clubs.

When the jump overcall is used to show a sound suit without side strength, it follows that the simple overcall tends to be a somewhat better hand.

In responding to your partner's jump overcall, don't seriously consider a game unless you have a magnificent distributional fit or about 16 points in high-card strength. Don't rescue him unless you are almost positive that your suit is better than his.

THE OVERCALL IN NOTRUMP

An overcall of one notrump shows a hand of about the same value as an opening bid of one notrump: 16 to 18 points, with balanced distribution, and at least three suits stopped. In this case, you *guarantee* at least one stopper in the enemy's bid suit.

Partner should respond to it much as he does to an opening bid of one notrump: a takeout at the level of two is weak, a jump to three of a suit is strong, a raise to two notrump is invitational.

The Stayman Convention is not recommended in this situation. In most cases, the responder can get information if he makes a cue bid in the enemy's bid suit.

South	West	North	East
1 ♡	1 NT	Pass	2 ♡

East's cue bid is forcing to game, and West is expected to show a major suit if he has one.

THE TRAP PASS

When an opponent bids a suit in which you have length and strength, it usually pays to pass. This kind of pass is often called a *trap* pass.

Many opponents will bid more energetically when you keep silent. Presumably, they will get into trouble, and you will reap the harvest for your patience.

True, good opponents are not likely to bid wildly just because nobody has opposed them. However, even opponents who know the value of their cards may make the overbid rather than the underbid in a borderline case when uncontested.

The chief reason for passing when you have length in the enemy's suit is to stay out of trouble. If you and the bidder have nine or more cards in a suit, very few cards of that suit are left for the remaining two players. The bidder's partner will be short and will be looking for a chance to get out of trouble. If you overcall, he may be only too happy to double for penalties!

South	West	North	East
1 ♡	?		

500. ♠ K Q J 7 5   ♡ K J 7 4 3   ◊ 8 4   ♣ 3

Pass. At best, there is very little future if you get into the auction, but you may collect a neat profit with the pass. North, who is surely short in hearts, may flounder around in the attempt to find a safer spot — he may even bid spades! In that case, your spade overcall would have been *disastrous!*

THE TAKEOUT DOUBLE

The takeout double asks partner to bid his best suit. You employ the double when your hand is strong enough to call for some action; when you are short in the enemy's suit; and when you are ready for any suit your partner names (or when you are prepared to name a very strong suit of your own).

The normal takeout double shows a singleton or void in the enemy's suit (sometimes a doubleton) with at least 12 points in high-card strength. It is sound to make a takeout double with far greater strength; you will find a strong rebid. It is occasionally desirable to make a takeout double with a slightly weaker hand, particularly when not vulnerable against vulnerable opponents; the idea is to get into the auction and find a fit at a low level.

Except for this rather rare weak takeout double in favorable vulnerability (often made when the hand is not quite solid enough for a good overcall), the double indicates that game is quite possible.

Because the takeout double strongly suggests game, it should guarantee length and strength in at least one unbid major suit. When you double a major suit, you should always have strong support (usually good *four*-card support) for the unbid major.

For example, consider the following hands after an opening bid of one heart on your right:

501. ♠ K J 9 4   ♡ 6   ◇ K 8 3 2   ♣ A J 7 5
Double. Ideal distribution for a takeout double, with 12 points in high cards, well distributed among the unbid suits.

502. ♠ 6   ♡ K J 9 4   ◇ K 8 3 2   ♣ A J 7 5
Pass. You would double an opening bid of one spade, but you mustn't even dream of doubling one heart. This is just the spot for a trap pass.

503. ♠ Q J 9 4   ♡ 6   ◇ Q 8 3 2   ♣ A J 7 5
Pass. The right distribution, but not enough strength for a takeout double.

504. ♠ K J 9   ♡ 6 3   ◇ K 8 3 2   ♣ A J 7 5
Pass. Avoid a 12-point takeout double unless you have the ideal distribution.

505. ♠ K J 9   ♡ 6 3   ◇ K Q 3 2   ♣ A J 7 5
Double. The distribution is not ideal, but your 14 points call for some action. You would be better pleased with 4-card support for the unbid major.

506. ♠ K Q 3 2   ♡ 6 3   ◇ K J 9   ♣ A J 7 5
Double. You prefer this hand to the previous one.

507. ♠ A Q 9 2   ♡ 6   ◇ K Q J 2   ♣ A K 7 5
Double. This hand is, of course, far stronger than No. 501. You will indicate the difference by the strength of your rebid.

RESPONDING TO A TAKEOUT DOUBLE

The responder makes a minimum bid with 0 to 8 points. He should think about game with 9 points or more. The combined total will be only about 21 points if the doubler has a minimum double, but doubler's singleton in the enemy's suit will help. Moreover, the doubler may have a point or two more than a bare minimum.

The responder should virtually insist on a game when he has 11 points or more.

The responder can invite a game by making a jump bid in his best suit. This jump response is highly invitational, but not forcing. In order to force, the responder makes a cue bid in the enemy's bid suit.

The responder passes the takeout double for penalties only when he has a long and very solid holding in the trump suit. He should want his partner to lead trumps, and he should expect to lead trumps himself at every opportunity. A good player does not pass a takeout double just because he has a weak hand. *The weaker the hand,* goes the old rule, *the more essential the takeout.*

Given a choice, the responder will bid a major rather than a minor suit. If his only long suit is that bid by the enemy, the responder may be able to bid notrump (which shows some scattered strength) or may have to respond in his cheapest 3-card suit.

For example:

South	West	North	East
1 ♡	Double	Pass	?

508. ♠ 7 6 5 2   ♡ 9 8 4   ◇ J 7 5   ♣ 9 3 2

Bid one spade. The weaker the hand, the more essential the takeout.

509. ♠ 7 6 5   ♡ 9 8 4 3   ◇ J 7 5   ♣ 9 3 2

Bid one spade. Bid the cheapest 3-card suit in this situation.

510. ♠ Q J 5 2   ♡ 8 4 3   ◇ K 7 5   ♣ 9 3 2

Bid one spade. You can make only a minimum response, but you are far from despondent. If partner extends a game invitation, you will gladly accept.

511. ♠ Q 9 7 6 2   ♡ 8 4 3   ◇ K 7 5   ♣ A 4

Bid two spades. The jump response shows about 9 or 10 points in high cards and invites the doubler to go on towards game.

512. ♠ Q J 5 2   ♡ 8 4   ◇ K 5   ♣ 1 0 9 7 3 2

Bid one spade. Respond in the 4-card major rather than in the weak 5-card minor.

513. ♠ Q J 5 2   ♡ 8   ◇ A J 7 5   ♣ K 9 3 2

Bid two hearts. The cue bid in the enemy's suit is forcing to game. If partner bids spades, as you expect, you will raise to four spades.

514. ♠ Q J 5   ♡ 8   ◇ A J 7 5 3   ♣ K 9 3 2

Bid two hearts. If partner bids spades, you will then show your diamonds. You will raise the spades if they are rebid, but otherwise you will consider game in a minor suit.

515. ♠ 7 5   ♡ Q J 8 4   ◇ K 7 5   ♣ J 9 3 2

Bid one notrump. This bid shows at least one stopper in the enemy's suit with some slight smattering of strength. Do not make this response with something like Q-J-x-x in the enemy's suit and no other strength in the hand.

516. ♠ 7 5   ♡ Q J 8 4 2   ◇ K 7 5   ♣ J 9 3

Bid one notrump. Your hearts are not solid enough for a penalty pass.

517. ♠ 7   ♡ Q J 1 0 8 4   ◇ K 7 5   ♣ J 9 3 2

Pass. You want to have trumps led as often as possible, and your heart holding is solid enough for this purpose.

THE DOUBLER'S REBIDS

When the responder has bid only a minimum, he may have a perfectly ghastly hand. You have forced him to bid, and he has obeyed orders. The doubler must avoid getting the responder into further trouble.

A good rule to follow in such situations is to give your partner credit for about one queen and one jack, together with four cards in the suit of his response. Then bid what you think can be made if he has some such nearly worthless hand.

You will usually have to pass a minimum response. Sometimes you will be able to raise from one to two of a suit. Rarely will you be able to go to the level of three. Practically never will your hand be good enough for a jump to game.

In the series of hands Nos. 501 to 507, only the last was worth further action over partner's minimum response of one spade. With No. 507, you would raise a conservative partner to four spades, but you would raise a good aggressive partner to only three spades.

When the doubler makes a rebid in his own suit at the level of one, he doesn't necessarily guarantee a very strong hand.

South	West	North	East
1 ◊	Double	Pass	1 ♡
Pass	1 ♠		

West should not have a minimum hand, but he may not have a really strong double.

When the doubler rebids in his own suit at the level of *two,* he shows a very strong hand. He needs about two kings or so for game.

South	West	North	East
1 ◊	Double	Pass	1 ♠
Pass	2 ♡		

West should have some such hand as:

518.   ♠ A 8 4   ♡ A K J 10 7 3   ◊ 5   ♣ Q J 3

If the doubler makes a jump rebid in his own suit, his bid is either highly invitational or forcing, depending on whether his suit is a major or a minor.

South	West	North	East
1 ♦	Double	Pass	1 ♡
Pass	3 ♣		

West undoubtedly has a fit for hearts and is making the jump bid in clubs on his way to game. This bid is forcing.

South	West	North	East
1 ♦	Double	Pass	2 ♣
Pass	3 ♠		

Highly invitational, but not completely forcing. West must have a fine spade suit and a magnificent hand, but if he could guarantee a game all by himself he would have bid two diamonds at his first turn.

THE CUE BID IN THE ENEMY'S SUIT

The surest way to force to game after an opponent's opening bid is to make a cue bid in the enemy's suit.

South	West	North	East
1 ♡	2 ♡		

This is equivalent to a gigantic takeout double, forcing to game. West should have some such hand as:

519. ♠ K Q J 7 4   ♡ —   ◊ A K Q 6   ♣ K Q 10 9

In a pinch, this bid may be made with a singleton in the enemy's suit rather than the promised void.

Sometimes a player doubles for a takeout and then bids the enemy's suit:

South	West	North	East
1 ◊	Double	Pass	1 ♡
Pass	2 ◊		

At one time, this was used to show a real diamond suit and was called "exposing the psychic." No modern expert uses it for this purpose today. The cue bid is used as a way of forcing to game and shows an extremely good fit with the response.

QUIZ No. 41

North	East	South	West
1 ♠	?		

Neither side is vulnerable.

520. ♠ 5   ♡ K Q 7 3   ◇ A Q 3 2   ♣ 10 9 4 3
521. ♠ 9 5 4   ♡ K Q 10 9 3   ◇ Q 10 9 7   ♣ 3
522. ♠ 7 4   ♡ A Q 9 6 3   ◇ Q 9 2   ♣ A 7 3
523. ♠ 8 4   ♡ 6 2   ◇ K Q 10 8 5 2   ♣ K J 2
524. ♠ 10 3   ♡ A K Q J 7 4   ◇ K Q 2   ♣ K 5
525. ♠ K J 8 6 2   ♡ A 2   ◇ A 7 5   ♣ A 10 3
526. ♠ A Q J 9   ♡ 6   ◇ A Q J 9 8   ♣ 10 5 2
527. ♠ A J 8   ♡ A Q 7 3   ◇ K 5   ♣ Q 10 8 2
528. ♠ A J 8   ♡ A Q   ◇ K 10 6 2   ♣ Q 10 8 2
529. ♠ —   ♡ Q 10 2   ◇ A Q J 9 6 2   ♣ K 10 4 2
530. ♠ —   ♡ A J 10 2   ◇ A K J 8 6   ♣ K Q J 9
531. ♠ 8   ♡ K Q J 10 9 3   ◇ A 10 9 2   ♣ K Q

QUIZ No. 42

The bidding is the same as in Quiz No. 41, but both sides are vulnerable. What do you bid on each of the same twelve hands?

QUIZ No. 43

The bidding is the same as in Quiz No. 41, but this time you are vulnerable and the opponents are not. What do you bid on each of the twelve hands?

QUIZ No. 44

The bidding is the same as in Quiz No. 41, but this time you are not vulnerable and the opponents are. What do you bid on each of the twelve hands?

QUIZ No. 45

	North	East	South	West
	1 ◇	Double	Pass	?

	♠	♡	◇	♣
532.	♠ 8 7 5 2	♡ 6 3	◇ 10 8 7 5 2	♣ K 4
533.	♠ Q 5	♡ J 9 7 6	◇ 8 2	♣ K 8 6 4 2
534.	♠ A K 7 4	♡ J 3	◇ J 6 2	♣ 10 6 5 2
535.	♠ A 5	♡ K J 10 6 4 2	◇ 7 2	♣ Q 8 3
536.	♠ A K 7 4 3	♡ Q 4	◇ 10 6 2	♣ 8 7 4
537.	♠ A Q 10 5 3	♡ A J 3	◇ 7 3 2	♣ Q 4
538.	♠ 9 6 4	♡ Q 8 2	◇ A Q	♣ 9 7 6 3 2
539.	♠ 10 7 5	♡ 9 4 2	◇ 10 8 3 2	♣ Q 7 3

QUIZ No. 46

	North	East	South	West
	1 ◇	Double	Pass	1 ♠
	Pass	?		

	♠	♡	◇	♣
540.	♠ K Q 3 2	♡ A 6 4	◇ 9 2	♣ K 8 3 2
541.	♠ A Q 3	♡ A Q 8 4 2	◇ 8	♣ J 8 4 2
542.	♠ K Q 2	♡ A Q J 9 7 3	◇ 4	♣ A K 3
543.	♠ Q 10 4	♡ A Q J 8 3	◇ A J 10	♣ K 4
544.	♠ Q J 9 4	♡ A Q J 9 8	◇ 3	♣ A K 4

9. Competitive Bidding

When both sides are in the auction, it is sometimes difficult to tell whose hand it is. It is also sometimes difficult to know when to double and when to bid more of your own side's suit.

There are no easy answers to these questions. Experts often fail to find the right solutions. A knowledge of the principles and of the players in your game will help you find the right answers in practice.

THE FREE RAISE

After an opponent's overcall, you are not under pressure to keep your partner's bid open. He will get a second chance to speak even if you pass.

For this reason, it is often thought that you should promise substantial values for the competitive (usually called *free*) raise. For example:

South	West	North	East
1 ♡	2 ♣	2 ♡	

What does North need for this free raise? Set the requirements too low, and the bid is meaningless. Set them too high, and North loses the chance to show support at a low level. Moreover, East has a cheap chance to bid if North passes, but may lose this chance if North bids.

An acceptable compromise distinguishes between minor and major suits. It is sound to raise a major suit with a light hand (7 or 8 points) provided that you have good trump support. You need slightly more, however (about 8 to 10 points), for the raise of a minor suit. The theory is that the major suit has a more pre-emptive effect and provides a shorter road to game. You need more to raise a minor suit because there is little if any pre-emptive effect and because game is much more remote.

In the situation described, the free raise to two hearts might be as weak as:

545. ♠ 8 3   ♡ Q 8 6 4   ◊ K Q 7 3   ♣ 7 3 2

It might be as strong as:

546. ♠ K Q 7 3   ♡ Q 8 6 4   ◊ A 3   ♣ 7 3 2
This is an extreme case.

547. ♠ A 3   ♡ Q 8 6 4   ◊ K Q 7 3   ♣ 7 3 2
Bid two diamonds over the overcall of two clubs. You will raise hearts later thus showing the full value of your hand.

THE FREE TAKEOUT IN A NEW SUIT

As we have seen, the standard takeout in a new suit makes a sharp distinction between the cheap takeout at the level of one and the more expensive takeout at the level of two. The same principle operates in the case of the *free* response.

If you can make your response at the level of one, particularly in a suit of five or more cards, you need very little more than minimum values. If you must make your response at the level of two, you need full values, just as if there had been no overcall. If you must make your overcall at the level of three, or if your suit is higher than partner's suit and is made at the level of two, you need a very good hand indeed. Takeouts and rebids at the level of three (or at the "reverse" level) should practically guarantee game at some contract.

South	West	North	East
1 ◊	1 ♡	?	

548. ♠ K J 9 7 4   ♡ 8   ◊ Q 7 5 4   ♣ 8 5 3
Bid one spade. There are only 6 points in high cards, but

the distribution is good, and the diamond fit is a good guarantee that some safe contract exists.

549. ♠ 8 5 3   ♡ 8   ◇ Q 7 5 4   ♣ K J 9 7 4

Bid two diamonds. The hand is not strong enough for a takeout to two clubs, whether the opponent overcalls or passes. The hand is a shade light for a free raise to two diamonds, but most experts would make this raise nevertheless.

South	West	North	East
1 ♠	2 ◇	?	

550. ♠ 8 4 3   ♡ K Q J 6 3   ◇ 8 4   ♣ A 5 2

Bid two hearts. You can make the same bid that you would have made if West had passed.

551. ♠ 8 4 3   ♡ A 5 2   ◇ 8 4   ♣ K Q J 6 3

Bid two spades. You cannot afford to bid the clubs at the level of three. As a compromise, you must raise spades — not because you are delighted to do so with three small trumps but because you would be even less pleased to pass this hand.

552. ♠ 8 4   ♡ A 5 2   ◇ 8 4 3   ♣ K Q J 6 3

Pass. You cannot raise spades with a doubleton, and you cannot afford to bid three clubs. No other bid is available so you must pass. This is very awkward, but the chances are that your partner will reopen the bidding and thus give you a chance to show your strength.

FREE REBIDS BY THE OPENER

In some competitive auctions it is quite clear that both sides are jockeying for the part score. In others, it is possible that one or both sides are aiming at game. It isn't possible to clarify this completely because some situations are bound to be confusing. It is possible, however, to indicate what principles should guide you.

When the bidding is dropped at a part score, either partner may make a further bid as a competitive measure without fearing that he will be taken too seriously:

South	West	North	East
1 ♠	2 ♡	2 ♠	Pass
Pass	3 ♡	3 ♠	

North is just competing, not trying for a game. South would be guilty of a breach of partnership confidence if he now went on to four spades (unless he had a very remarkable hand).

Unless North is allowed this kind of latitude in such situations, he must either allow the enemy to play the hand at three hearts or find himself in *four* spades. It is only logical that there must be *some* way for the hand to be played at only *three* spades.

Similarly, if North passed over three hearts, South could bid three spades with every confidence that North will pass.

Our next case is not so clear:

South	West	North	East
1 ♠	2 ♡	2 ♠	3 ♡
3 ♠			

Is South just competing, or is he inviting North to bid a game?

The only sure thing is that South cannot bid four spades all by himself. If he could, he would. (In some very delicate bidding situations, even this isn't true. A player sometimes bids less than the full value of his hand, expecting to be "pushed" by the enemy. The idea is to coax the enemy into doubling or to persuade them not to take a cheap sacrifice against what sounds like a very shaky game contract.)

South should definitely have more than a minimum opening bid. With a bare minimum he could afford to pass and leave further competition, if any, to his partner.

In short, South should have more than a minimum but

not enough for game. Conceivably, he would have bid three spades even if the intervening player had passed — clearly inviting a game. Conceivably, he has a shade less than this strength.

Some experts set up very strict requirements for a free rebid in this situation, but for most players such rules are made only to be broken.

ACTION OVER A TAKEOUT DOUBLE

What should you do when your partner's opening bid has been doubled for a takeout?

With a hopeless hand, pass.

Raise lightly to two of partner's suit. With the normal sound raise, jump to three of his suit. The raise to four is much the same whether or not the takeout double has been made.

Bid one notrump with 9 scattered points or so.

Redouble with any *very* good hand (12 points or more), particularly with support for partner's suit. You can later show the support for partner's suit at two, three, or four — depending on your full value.

Bid a new suit with a mediocre hand and a fairly good suit. If you fail to act promptly, it may be too expensive to bid later on. You will then have to guess whether to stay tamely out of the auction or barge wildly in.

FREE RESPONSES TO THE TAKEOUT DOUBLE

Suppose your partner has doubled the opening bid for a takeout. The next player has raised, bid, or redoubled. You are relieved of the responsibility of bidding. If you have a very weak hand, you can afford to pass.

South	West	North	East
1 ♡	Double	2 ♡	?

553. ♠ J 9 6 3   ♡ 8 5 4   ◇ Q 8 5 3   ♣ 7 2

Pass. If partner has a very good hand, he can double again (likewise for a takeout). If he has only a moderately good hand, he can sell out.

554. ♠ Q J 9 6 3　　♡ 8 5 4　　◇ Q 8 5 3　　♣ 7

Bid two spades. It is all right to stretch a trifle to respond freely to the takeout double. In this case you have a good spade suit and fine distribution.

The same principles apply if North redoubles. East should pass with a bad hand, allowing his partner to get himself out of trouble. East can afford to bid any five-card suit if he takes up no bidding room in the process; but he should avoid getting in the way with a bad hand if he thereby deprives his partner of a safe bid.

South	West	North	East
1 ◇	Double	Redouble	?

555. ♠ 8 5　　♡ 9 7 5 3 2　　◇ 8 4　　♣ 6 5 2

Bid one heart. This is an extreme case, but the bid is proper. If partner doesn't like hearts, he can bid what he was going to bid if you hadn't stepped in. Your bid has consumed no room.

556. ♠ 8 5　　♡ 6 5 2　　◇ 8 4　　♣ Q 7 5 3 2

Pass. Do not bid two clubs, since that would stop your partner from finding a safe haven at one heart or one spade. A bid of two clubs consumes bidding room.

557. ♠ 8 5　　♡ 6 5 2　　◇ 8 4　　♣ K Q 7 5 3

Bid two clubs. A free bid in this situation promises strength if it uses up bidding room.

THE LIGHT DOUBLE

At low levels, the penalty double is a kind of free bid. Take this situation:

South	West	North	East
1 ♠	2 ◇	?	

558. ♠ 7 3   ♡ K J 8 5   ◊ Q J 8 5   ♣ A 10 3

North can hardly pass with 11 good points in high cards. He cannot raise spades with a doubleton. He is not anxious to bid the broken 4-card heart suit. He cannot bid two notrump because that would show 13 to 15 points.

North should double for penalties.

This kind of double shows sound values for a free bid, including strength in the enemy's suit. The more trump strength, the less outside strength is needed; and vice versa.

An example of a light double with a poor trump holding:

559. ♠ 7 3   ♡ A Q 8 5   ◊ J 8 5   ♣ A Q 10 3

You would still double two diamonds even though you lack a sure trump trick.

It follows that your partner must use his discretion about letting such doubles stand. In the old Webster cartoons, the worst sinner was the player who took his partner out of a penalty double. Most experts cheerfully sin in this way — and their partners expect them to do so!

Let your partner's double stand when your hand is well equipped for defense. Take the double out when your hand is bad for defense.

South	West	North	East
1 ♠	2 ◊	Double	Pass
?			

560. ♠ A K J 7 4   ♡ K J 7   ◊ 9 3   ♣ K 8 3

Pass. You expect to take your full share of tricks on defense. With any sort of luck, you should collect a juicy penalty.

561. ♠ A K J 8 4 2   ♡ J 7 3   ◊ 3   ♣ K 8 3

Bid two spades. You have very little defense, and most of your strength is in a six-card suit.

562. ♠ A K Q J 8 4 2   ♡ J 7 3   ◊ 3   ♣ K 8

Bid three spades. You are ill equipped for defense, but magnificently ready for offense. The jump bid shows the difference.

563. ♠ K Q J 8 4   ♡ K Q J 7 3   ◇ —   ♣ K 8 3

Bid two hearts. Ill equipped for defense, but the chances are that your partner can raise hearts.

An important item to remember is that the penalty double of two diamonds (or any lower contract) is not too dangerous even if it misfires. The opponents do not score game for making two diamonds doubled.

When you double two hearts, or any higher contract, you must be somewhat surer of your ground. It still isn't necessary to have the kind of double that your banker would lend money on; just have the upper range of the light doubles we have just been discussing.

What do you say when the player at your right overcalls in the suit that you were about to bid? Double if you have a good hand; but pass if your only strength is in the enemy's suit.

The reason for the restraint is very simple. Why warn the enemy of danger when they're in the only spot that you can damage? When you have considerable length in the enemy's suit, both his partner and yours will be short in that suit; and one of them usually rescues if you double.

You don't always lose the chance to penalize the enemy when you pass in this situation. Your partner sometimes reopens the bidding with a double (for takeout) and then you are happy to pass for penalties.

LEAD-DIRECTING DOUBLES

At high levels, certain doubles are meant to indicate a favorable opening lead. This is particularly true of game contracts in notrumps, of slams, and of cue bids.

When you double a notrump contract, particularly game or higher, you request an opening lead:

In your own suit, if you have bid (whether or not your partner has also bid);

In partner's suit if he has made the only bid for your side;

In the first suit bid by the dummy if your side has not bid or doubled.

South	West	North	East
1 ◇	1 ♠	2 ◇	2 ♡
2 NT	Pass	3 NT	Double

East's double requests a lead in hearts, his own bid suit. He should have some such hand as:

564. ♠ 5 3   ♡ K Q J 10 7   ◇ A 3   ♣ 10 9 5 3

East expects to establish his hearts if the suit is led at once. He will gain the lead with the ace of diamonds in time to set the contract.

East should be cautious of doubling with any side ace but that in the enemy's suit. Conceivably, South may make the contract if he is allowed to run a long minor suit together with a couple of side aces.

South	West	North	East
1 ◇	1 ♠	3 ◇	Pass
3 NT	Pass	Pass	Double

East's double requests a lead in spades, the only suit bid by his side. He should have some such hand as:

565. ♠ Q 10 4   ♡ 7 4 3   ◇ J 10 9 5   ♣ 8 3 2

West must have a broken spade suit from which he may be very reluctant to lead. The double tells him to lead his suit. East expects to help establish the spades quickly, after which West should be able to gain the lead in hearts or clubs in time to defeat the contract. East's stopper in diamonds gives him some insurance against a long solid suit. This double is somewhat shaky, but it offers by far the best chance to defeat the contract.

South	West	North	East
1 ♠	Pass	2 ◊	Pass
2 NT	Pass	3 NT	Double
Pass	Pass	Pass	

East's double requests a lead in diamonds, the first (in this case the *only*) suit bid by the dummy. East may have:

566. ♠ 7 3 2   ♡ 6 4   ◊ K Q J 9   ♣ K Q 4 3

With a diamond opening lead, East hopes to set up three diamond tricks and an eventual club. In the meantime, moreover, West is steered away from a probable heart opening lead which might well cost a trick.

These doubles may well boomerang, but at rubber bridge they will gain points in the long run. Declarer can seldom if ever afford to redouble and will seldom make his contract. If he gains 150 points occasionally because of the double, he will lose far more in the long run when his contract is defeated by the killing lead.

SLAM DOUBLES

The double of a slam contract asks for an *unusual* lead. Some experts call rigidly for the first suit bid by the dummy, but this is too confining. The better procedure is to ask for a thoughtful and unusual lead, allowing the opener to use his judgment to a slight extent.

The theory is that you won't get rich doubling slams that have been bid by reliable opponents. You will usually beat the contract one trick, if at all, and the double will produce only 50 or 100 points more than a mere pass.

The double is reserved, instead, to ask for a lead that improves your chance to defeat a contract that would otherwise be made. This is worth about 1,000 or 1,500 points, depending on vulnerability. Even if your double doesn't produce results every single time, it will still be a winning call.

Most slam doubles are based on ruffing power. You ask your partner to lead the suit of which you are void (he can usually guess the suit from the bidding or from his own length), so that you can ruff at once. Presumably you have some other sure or probable trick for your double, since one ruffing trick will not defeat the slam.

In rare cases, it is necessary to take your tricks quickly against a slam before declarer can get his discards. The slam double may then indicate the right suit (an *unusual* suit) to begin with.

Before we can discuss the unusual lead, we must first settle on what leads are usual against a slam. It is customary for your partner to lead your suit if you have bid one, or his suit if he has bid one, or an unbid suit if only the opponents have bid.

Don't double if the *usual* lead will defeat the contract. Your double will then steer your partner to a different opening lead, and this may hurt your chance to defeat the slam. In the absence of a double, your partner will tend to make a lead in the *usual* suit on the theory that you may be ready to defeat the slam with this lead.

South	West	North	East
1 ♡	Pass	2 ♠	Pass
3 ♡	Pass	5 ♡	Pass
6 ♡	Pass	Pass	?

567. ♠ ——   ♡ 7 3 2   ◇ A 8 5 3 2   ♣ K Q 8 6 4

Double. You hope to ruff a spade opening lead and then cash the ace of diamonds. If spades are not led, declarer may draw trumps and discard his losers on dummy's good spades.

568. ♠ 7 4   ♡ 7 3 2   ◇ A 8 5 3   ♣ A 8 6 4

Pass. You hope to take both of your aces, and you want your partner to lead one of the unbid suits. If you double, he will lead a spade, and you may then lose one or both of the aces!

DOUBLING A CUE BID

It is sometimes advisable to double a cue bid (or a response to Blackwood) to indicate a favorable opening lead. For example:

South	West	North	East
1 ♠	Pass	3 ♠	Pass
4 ♣	Pass	4 ♡	Double

North doesn't intend to play the hand at hearts, so there is no chance that the double will be left in. East should indicate good hearts, headed by at least K-Q:

569. ♠ 7 3   ♡ K Q 9 7 4   ◇ 8 5 3   ♣ 7 5 3

East welcomes a heart opening lead and cannot support any other opening lead.

570. ♠ 7 3   ♡ Q 10 9 7 5 4 2   ◇ 5 3   ♣ 7 3

Pass. There is no advantage in doubling the hearts for penalties. The enemy will not stay there, and you will only persuade your partner that you can support a heart opening lead.

A player's *failure* to double a cue bid may be the decisive clue in the selection of the best opening lead:

South	West	North	East
1 ♠	Pass	3 ♠	Pass
4 ♣	Pass	4 ♡	Pass
6 ♠	Pass	Pass	Pass

West will tend not to lead hearts on the theory that his partner might have doubled the cue bid if he held heart strength. West will therefore tend to lead a diamond, or perhaps even a club.

LATE COMPETITIVE DOUBLES

When both sides bid up to a high level, you must often decide whether to double the opponents or to make a further bid of your own. A third possibility, often neglected in these situations, is the *forcing pass.*

The first question to settle is whether or not the hand *clearly* belongs to your side. If it does, you can afford to double with reasonable defensive strength; bid with offensive strength; and pass with indeterminate hands.

South	West	North	East
1 ♠	2 ♡	3 ♠	4 ♡
4 ♠	Pass	Pass	5 ♡
?			

571. ♠ A K J 7 5   ♡ Q J 5   ◊ K Q 7   ♣ 8 3

Double. Part of your strength is in the enemy's suit.

572. ♠ A K J 7 5 3   ♡ 8   ◊ K Q J 7   ♣ K 3

Bid five spades. You have considerable extra *offensive* strength and should be safe at this contract.

573. ♠ A K J 7 5   ♡ 8 5   ◊ K Q 7   ♣ Q J 5

Pass. Your hand is neither clearly offensive nor clearly defensive. You can afford to turn the problem over to your partner. Your pass forces him to double or bid on. (It is therefore called a *forcing pass*.)

In situations of this sort, when the opponents are sound bidders, it usually pays to bid on, rather than make a very doubtful double. The distribution is often very weird when the bidding is competitive up to a high level, and it may well turn out that whichever side wins the auction will make its contract! The difference between making your own game and allowing the enemy to make a game is more than a thousand points.

PART-SCORE BIDDING

The presence of a part score may seriously affect your bidding, whether the score is yours or the enemy's.

If the part score is yours, you have the chance to score a full game on a hand that is not game-going in its own right. If the opponents compete in the effort to stop you from making a cheap game, you have the chance to double them for penalties — after which you will *still* have the part score for the next hand.

As a result, you tend to open somewhat light in any position when your side has a part score of 40 points or more. (A part score of only 30 points is seldom much help; and a part score of only 20 points should be virtually ignored.) This process of lightening can be applied to opening suit bids of one, opening bids of one notrump, and opening suit bids of two.

574. ♠ K Q 7 5 3   ♡ A 8 6   ◊ Q 8 5   ♣ 7 3

Bid one spade in any position when your side has a part score of 40 or more. You will pass two hearts, will raise two diamonds if necessary, or will bid two spades.

575. ♠ K Q 7   ♡ A 8 6   ◊ Q 8 5   ♣ K 7 3 2

Bid one notrump in any position when your side has a part score of 40 points or more. Partner may be able to steal the hand for two or three of his best suit. If the opponents compete, partner should make allowance for a balanced 14-point hand when considering a penalty double.

576. ♠ 7 3   ♡ A J 10 8 5   ◊ A K Q 8 5   ♣ A

Bid two hearts with a part score. You are willing to get up to three diamonds or three hearts even if partner has a poor hand. You want to suggest a slam if he has a good hand.

When the part score belongs to the opponents, you tend to pass a doubtful hand in fourth position for fear of stirring up the animals. In third position, you tend to pass a hand with broken suits but to bid a borderline hand with a strong suit. In first or second position you tend to open light on the theory that it pays to get in the first punch when the situation is competitive. The light notrump is even more essential when the part score belongs to the enemy; it tells your partner that he can expect help in any suit that he wants to compete in. The light opening two-bid is not necessary, however.

QUIZ No. 47

	North	East	South	West
	1 ◇	1 ♡	?	

577.	♠ 10 6 4 2	♡ 9 4 2	◇ J 3	♣ K Q 7 6
578.	♠ K J 8 7 3	♡ 10 4	◇ J 6 5	♣ Q J 3
579.	♠ 8 7	♡ Q J 9 8 6 5	◇ 4 2	♣ 8 6 3
580.	♠ J 6 2	♡ A Q	◇ 7 6 2	♣ K 10 9 5 3
581.	♠ K 9 6 5	♡ 7 3	◇ K Q 4 2	♣ Q 5 2

QUIZ No. 48

	North	East	South	West
	1 ♠	2 ♡	2 ♠	3 ♡
	?			

582.	♠ K Q J 6 3	♡ 7 4	◇ A J 3	♣ Q 10 4
583.	♠ K Q J 6 3	♡ 5	◇ A J 3	♣ Q 10 9 2
584.	♠ K Q J 6 3	♡ 5	◇ A J 3	♣ K J 10 6
585.	♠ K Q J 6 3	♡ 5	◇ A Q 3	♣ A J 10 5
586.	♠ K Q J 6 3	♡ 5	◇ K Q J	♣ A K Q 5

QUIZ No. 49

	North	East	South	West
	1 ♠	2 ♡	2 ♠	3 ♡
	3 ♠	Pass	?	

587.	♠ Q J 6 2	♡ 7 5	◇ A 10 6 4	♣ Q 9 3
588.	♠ K 9 8 4	♡ 7 5	◇ A 10 6 4	♣ Q J 4

QUIZ No. 50

	North	East	South	West
	1 ◇	1 NT	?	

589.	♠ Q 7 5	♡ 8 4	◇ K 10 3	♣ 10 9 5 3 2
590.	♠ Q 7 5	♡ 8 4	◇ K J 3	♣ A 10 8 6 5
591.	♠ K Q 10 8 3 2	♡ A 4	◇ J 7 3	♣ Q 5

592. ♠ 4   ♡ K J 10 8 6 2   ◇ 9 5 4   ♣ 8 3 2
593. ♠ Q 4   ♡ A Q J 10 2   ◇ 9 2   ♣ Q 6 5 2

QUIZ No. 51

North	East	South	West
1 ♡	2 ♣	?	

594. ♠ K J 9 6 3   ♡ 7 5 2   ◇ K 9 6   ♣ 4 3
595. ♠ K J 9 6 3   ♡ Q 9 3   ◇ K 9 6   ♣ 4 3
596. ♠ A J 10 5 2   ♡ Q 9 4   ◇ K J 6   ♣ 8 5
597. ♠ 10 8 6   ♡ A 6   ◇ K 9 4 2   ♣ Q 10 7 2
598. ♠ K J 5   ♡ K 7 6 3   ◇ A K Q 6 5 2   ♣ —
599. ♠ A 5 4   ♡ Q J 8 3   ◇ J 8 6 2   ♣ 7 4
600. ♠ K 5 4   ♡ Q 8 3 2   ◇ 10 8 2   ♣ 10 4 2
601. ♠ A J 8 4   ♡ Q J 7 3   ◇ K Q 2   ♣ 9 4

QUIZ No. 52

North	East	South	West
1 ♠	2 ♡	Pass	?

602. ♠ 9 5   ♡ 10 4 2   ◇ A K 7 6 3   ♣ Q 10 2
603. ♠ 10 5   ♡ Q 10 3 2   ◇ 5 4 3   ♣ K Q 8 2
604. ♠ 7   ♡ K 8 7 5   ◇ A K 5 3   ♣ A 8 5 2
605. ♠ Q 10 6 5   ♡ —   ◇ K Q 7 3 2   ♣ 10 8 7 5
606. ♠ A 3 2   ♡ Q 6   ◇ A 10 5 2   ♣ 9 8 6 4

QUIZ No. 53

North	East	South	West
1 ♡	Double	?	

Neither side is vulnerable.

607. ♠ A Q 10 8 3   ♡ Q 5   ◇ 10 8 3   ♣ K J 3
608. ♠ Q J 4   ♡ 9 6 3   ◇ K 8 4 2   ♣ 10 5 2
609. ♠ K Q 9 7 3   ♡ 8 5 2   ◇ Q 4 2   ♣ 8 3
610. ♠ Q 8 6   ♡ J 5 2   ◇ K 8 3   ♣ K 10 7 2

611.	♠ A Q 5	♡ K J 6 4 2	◇ 9 7	♣ Q J 3
612.	♠ K 7 5	♡ Q J 9 6 3	◇ 3	♣ 8 5 4 2
613.	♠ 8 6 2	♡ 7	◇ Q J 10 8 3	♣ 9 5 4 2
614.	♠ 8 2	♡ 4	◇ A K J 10 6 3	♣ K 8 4 2
615.	♠ 4 2	♡ 8 5	◇ K Q 10 9 7 2	♣ K 6 3
616.	♠ A 8 5 2	♡ K Q 3	◇ J 10 9 3	♣ 10 4

QUIZ No. 54

You are the dealer and have 60 on score. What do you bid?

617.	♠ K 7 3	♡ 10 3 2	◇ K 10 3	♣ A K J 2
618.	♠ A K Q 9 3	♡ A Q J 10 5	◇ A Q	♣ 3
619.	♠ K Q 3	♡ A K 5	◇ A Q 10 3	♣ A K 4
620.	♠ K Q J 9	♡ 10 4	◇ 9 6 5	♣ A K 9 3
621.	♠ A Q	♡ 10 8 2	◇ A J 6 2	♣ K 10 8 6

QUIZ No. 55

You are the dealer and your opponents have 60 on score.

622.	♠ 7 2	♡ K Q 8 7 2	◇ A J 9 6 4	♣ 4
623.	♠ J 10 3	♡ K 10 5	◇ A Q 7 2	♣ K J 10

QUIZ No. 56

North	East	South	West
1 ♡	Pass	?	

You have 60 on score and the bidding has proceeded:

624.	♠ 6 4	♡ Q 10 3	◇ A K J 7 2	♣ 6 5 3
625.	♠ Q 5	♡ 8 7	◇ J 6 3	♣ Q J 8 7 4 2
626.	♠ 8 5	♡ K Q 9 6	◇ A J 2	♣ A Q 8 3
627.	♠ A Q 6 5	♡ K Q 9 6	◇ A 8 3	♣ J 5
628.	♠ K 10 3	♡ J 2	◇ K J 8 3	♣ A J 9 2

10. The Play of the Cards

The play of the cards rates a book by itself.* This chapter will discuss some of the important plays that will help you in crucial situations. Answers to problems begin on page 184.

THE HOLD-UP

Most experienced players know about the hold-up play, but they don't realize how often it should be made. The familiar situation occurs when you have A-x-x of the suit that is led against you at notrump. You *hold up* your ace until the third trick (hence the name of the play) in the hope that one of the opponents will not be able to lead the suit if he later wins a trick.

This is correct, as far as it goes. We should add that the hold-up is unnecessary if you can take all of your tricks on the run. It is unwise if some other suit is more dangerous than the suit that has been led. And the hold-up is wrong if you have 10-x-x-x opposite A-x, since you may develop a second stopper (the ten) or may block the suit by winning the first trick. So much for the cases in which it is wrong to hold up.

The hold-up may be wise even if you have *two* stoppers in the enemy's suit. If you have to give up the lead twice, you are in much the same spot as giving up the lead once with only one stopper in the suit that has been led. Moreover, in giving up your two tricks, you must usually try to begin with the suit in which the dangerous opponent has an entry. This point is illustrated in Hand No. 629.

The hold-up sometimes forces you to take only one trick in a suit that might well produce a second trick if you didn't hold up.

---

* See *Watson's Classic Book on the Play of the Hand*, published by Sterling Publishing Co., Inc., 1958.

The question is whether the hold-up is more important than the second trick in the dangerous suit. This point is illustrated in Hand Nos. 630 and 631.

An entirely different reason for the hold-up is shown in Hand No. 632. This play occurs surprisingly often, but is seldom recognized.

Incidentally, the hold-up is not solely a notrump play. It is often wise to hold up *once* at a trump contract when you have A-x-x opposite three small cards. There is no advantage in holding up *twice* with this sort of holding. (It is often important, moreover, to avoid having your ace ruffed.)

One more word about the hold-up before leaving the subject. It is a defensive as well as an offensive play. When defending, you can often create serious problems for declarer if you refuse to take your ace on the first trick. This applies chiefly to the trump suit and to a strong side suit. In the unimportant suits you must usually take an ace when you have the chance to capture a high card with it.

629. West   East

    ♠ A K 6   ♠ 10 5

    ♡ K 10 5   ♡ Q J 9

    ◇ Q J 10 7   ◇ A 9 8 6 2

    ♣ A 5 2   ♣ K 10 3

West is declarer at 3 NT. North leads ♠ 4. How should West plan the play?

630. West   East

    ♠ K J 9   ♠ 8 4 2

    ♡ A 10 4   ♡ Q 6

    ◇ K Q 8 5   ◇ A 7

    ♣ 9 4 3   ♣ A Q J 10 7 2

West is declarer at 3 NT. North leads ♠ 6, and South plays ♠ Q. How should West plan the play?

631. West   East
    ♠ A Q 5   ♠ J 9 3
    ♡ K 7 4   ♡ Q 3
    ◇ Q 9 3 2   ◇ A J 10 8 4
    ♣ A Q J   ♣ K 10 5

West is declarer at 3 NT. North leads ♡ 6. How should
West plan the play?

632. West   East
    ♠ A K Q J 10 8 6   ♠ 2
    ♡ 7 4 3   ♡ A 6
    ◇ 3   ◇ K Q 7 5 4
    ♣ A 5   ♣ 9 7 6 3 2

West is declarer at 4 ♠. North leads ♡ K. How should
West plan the play?

SUIT ESTABLISHMENT

All experienced players are familiar with the idea of establishing a suit by taking one or two top cards and then ruffing out
the remaining stoppers held by the enemy. This theme is devel-
oped in Hand Nos. 633 through 638.

These hands are not difficult, but the exact timing of the
tricks is worth noting. It is often necessary, for example, to begin
the long suit before touching trumps. It is then possible to use the
trump suit as a way of getting from one hand to the other in
order to continue the ruffing-out process.

633. West   East
    ♠ A Q J 10 6 4   ♠ K 9 2
    ♡ A 5   ♡ 3 2
    ◇ K 6 4   ◇ 5 3 2
    ♣ 6 4   ◇ A K 7 5 3

West is declarer at 4 ♠. North leads ♡ Q. How should West plan the play?

634. West   East
   ♠ A 10 9 7 2   ♠ K 8 6
   ♡ A 8 2   ♡ 7 3
   ◊ A J 7 3   ◊ 8 5 2
   ♣ 7   ♣ A K 6 4 3

West is declarer at 4 ♠. North leads ♡ Q; South plays ♡ 6. How should West plan the play?

635. West   East
   ♠ K Q J 10 8 7 6   ♠ A 9 2
   ♡ A 5 2   ♡ Q 3
   ◊ 7   ◊ A Q 6 5 2
   ♣ A Q   ♣ J 10 9

West is declarer at 6 ♠. North leads ♡ 10, and South covers the queen with the king. How should West plan the play?

636. West   East
   ♠ A K 4 3   ♠ 9 8 6 2
   ♡ 9   ♡ K 10 6
   ◊ 5 2   ◊ A J 7 4 3
   ♣ A K J 6 3 2   ♣ 4

West is declarer at 4 ♠. North leads ◊ 8. How should West plan the play?

637. West   East
   ♠ A K Q 10 9 6 3   ♠ J 8 7 2
   ♡ A 6   ♡ Q 5
   ◊ A K J   ◊ 6 5 4 3 2
   ♣ A   ♣ K Q

West is declarer at 7 ♠. North leads ♡ J, and South covers the queen with the king. How should West plan the play?

638. West   East

  ♠ A K J 10 9 4   ♠ Q 3
  ♡ 4   ♡ A K J 6 3
  ♢ A 10   ♢ K Q J
  ♣ K J 5 3   ♣ 8 7 2

West is declarer at 6 ♠. North leads ♢ 7. How should West plan the play?

AVOIDANCE

Avoidance is the technique of keeping the dangerous opponent out of the lead. It is often possible to play a suit in such a way as to give up a trick to a specified opponent (when a trick must be lost in any case).

In other cases the problem is to play an unimportant suit in such a way as to give you an avoidance play in a key suit. This point is illustrated in Hand No. 643.

Sometimes the method is to time the suits in the right order. In Hand No. 642, for example, one sequence of plays is dangerous, and another sequence is quite safe.

639. West   East

  ♠ A K 8 4 3   ♠ Q J 5 2
  ♡ A 4   ♡ J 6 2
  ♢ K 5 3 2   ♢ 10 4
  ♣ 10 5   ♣ A Q J 9

West is declarer at 4 ♠. North leads ♡ K. How should West plan the play?

640. West   East

  ♠ A 4   ♠ K J 7 6
  ♡ K Q 5   ♡ 7 4
  ♢ A 4 3   ♢ K 6 5 2
  ♣ A K 9 5 2   ♣ Q 6 3

West is declarer at 3 NT. North leads ♡ J, and South plays the ♡ 2. How should West plan the play?

641. West   East
    ♠ K J 9 8 6   ♠ A 10 7 4
    ♡ K 6 3   ♡ 5 4 2
    ◇ Q 9 2   ◇ A K J 8
    ♣ A K   ♣ 8 4

West is declarer at 4 ♠. North leads ◇ 7. How should West plan the play?

642. West   East
    ♠ A Q 7   ♠ J 4 2
    ♡ A J 5   ♡ K
    ◇ A 8 5   ◇ J 10 6 4
    ♣ Q 10 7 2   ♣ K J 9 8 3

West is declarer at 3 NT. North leads ♡ 6. How should West plan the play?

643. West   East
    ♠ A Q 10 7 5 4   ♠ K J 9
    ♡ 3   ♡ A 5
    ◇ K 6 3   ◇ 5 4 2
    ♣ 6 3 2   ♣ A K 7 5 4

West is declarer at 4 ♠. North leads ♡ K. How should West plan the play?

LOSER-ON-LOSER PLAYS

Few players have cultivated the art of losing tricks gracefully. Sometimes you can give up a trick at the least possible cost; and at other times you can give up one trick and get back two others.

In Hand No. 646, for example, the idea is to give up a sure

loser at a time when it will cost nothing. If you struggle, you will still give up the sure loser, and you may also lose an additional trick.

In No. 647, we have the same thought in a different setting. The idea of transferring a ruff from one suit to another may not strike you at first glance unless you become familiar with it.

In No. 644 and 645 we see the idea of giving up a trick in a suit that has no losers. Needless to say, you get back two tricks for the one trick that you give up.

In No. 648, the loser-on-loser idea may not develop if the diamonds break favorably. Advanced players, who make use of the end-play, know that it is often necessary to throw an opponent in the lead at the end with a loser-on-loser play.

644. | West | East |
|------|------|
| ♠ K Q J 10 9 3 | ♠ A 8 7 4 |
| ♡ A 9 4 | ♡ K 6 3 |
| ♢ A 8 3 2 | ♢ K 9 4 |
| ♣ — | ♣ K Q J |

West is declarer at 6 ♠. North leads ♡ Q. How should West plan the play?

645. | West | East |
|------|------|
| ♠ K 5 3 | ♠ — |
| ♡ A J 10 8 2 | ♡ K Q 9 7 6 4 |
| ♢ 5 4 | ♢ A K 3 2 |
| ♣ A Q 7 | ♣ 6 5 3 |

West is declarer at 6 ♡. North leads ♠ Q. How should West plan the play?

646. | West | East |
|------|------|
| ♠ K Q 10 7 6 5 | ♠ A 4 2 |
| ♡ 6 5 | ♡ 8 7 4 |
| ♢ A 7 | ♢ Q 10 8 5 3 |
| ♣ A Q J | ♣ K 10 |

West is declarer at 4 ♠, after South has opened the bidding with 1 ♡. North leads ♡ Q, and South takes two high hearts and leads a third heart. How should West plan the play?

647. West
- ♠ A K Q J 5
- ♡ 4 3
- ◇ A 4 2
- ♣ 7 6 3

East
- ♠ 7 6 3 2
- ♡ A K 6 2
- ◇ K 5 3
- ♣ Q 4

West is declarer at 4 ♠. (North has overcalled in clubs). North leads ♣ K, ♣ A, and ♣ J. How should West plan the play?

648. West
- ♠ A K 10 7 5 3
- ♡ K
- ◇ A K 6
- ♣ A Q 3

East
- ♠ Q J 9 8
- ♡ A Q
- ◇ 5 4 3 2
- ♣ 5 4 2

West is declarer at 6 ♠. North leads ◇ Q. (Trumps break 2-1.) How should West plan the play?

SAFETY PLAYS

The safety play, in its simplest form, is a way of playing a single suit to restrict the loss in that suit. It isn't always necessary to get the most out of a key suit; perhaps you can afford to give up one trick, *but not two,* in the suit. The safety play protects you against the loss that you cannot afford.

There is no general rule that guides you to the safety play. Your best plan is to familiarize yourself with the most common situations. When they come along at the table, as they often will, you will recognize them and will make the approved play.

When you have reached the stage of recognizing the more familiar safety plays and the situations in which they are needed, you will be ready to do your own thinking at the table. Then you will note at the beginning of a hand how many tricks you can afford to lose (without going down). You will look for plays that will hold the loss to what you can afford — and you will find yourself inventing safety plays that aren't in the books!

649. West   East
     ♠ A K 10 9 7 5   ♠ 6 3
     ♡ 5   ♡ 7 6 4 3
     ◊ A K 2   ◊ Q 6 3
     ♣ A K 5   ♣ 8 4 3 2

West is declarer at 4 ♠. North leads ♡ K and continues with ♡ Q. How should West plan the play?

650. West   East
     ♠ K 5   ♠ A J 8 3 2
     ♡ A K 10 5 3   ♡ 7 6 4
     ◊ A J 9 2   ◊ K Q 10
     ♣ A K   ♣ Q J

West is declarer at 6 NT. North leads ◊ 8. How should West plan the play?

651. West   East
     ♠ A J 6 4 2   ♠ K 9 5 3
     ♡ K Q 3 2   ♡ A J
     ◊ 6   ◊ A J 9 7 4
     ♣ A 5 3   ♣ K Q

West is declarer at 6 ♠. North leads ♣ J, and South plays ♣ 2. How should West plan the play?

652. West   East
     ♠ 6   ♠ K Q 5 2
     ♡ A J 10 9   ♡ K Q 7
     ◊ A K 6   ◊ 4 3
     ♣ A 8 7 3 2   ♣ K Q 9 6

West is declarer at 6 ♣. North leads ◊ Q. How should West plan the play?

653. West | East
♠ K Q 8 6 5 | ♠ J 4 3 2
♡ 5 4 2 | ♡ A K Q
◊ A K 3 | ◊ 5 4 2
♣ 7 3 | ♣ K Q 5

West is declarer at 4 ♠. North leads ♡ 8. How should West plan the play?

654. West | East
♠ A J 8 | ♠ 5 2
♡ A K 6 | ♡ 7 4 3
◊ 6 4 2 | ◊ A K 5
♣ A 9 5 2 | ♣ Q J 6 4 3

West is declarer at 3 NT. North leads ♡ Q. How should West plan the play?

655. West | East
♠ K 7 4 | ♠ A 3
♡ K 7 5 3 | ♡ A 6 2
◊ K 9 4 | ◊ A J 5 3 2
♣ A Q 3 | ♣ 7 6 2

West is declarer at 3 NT. North leads ♠ Q. How should West plan the play?

656. West | East
♠ A Q 5 | ♠ K J 3
♡ A Q 7 6 4 2 | ♡ 5 3
◊ 7 | ◊ Q 10 6
♣ J 5 3 | ♣ A K Q 4 2

West is declarer at 4 ♡. North leads ◊ K and then shifts to ♠ 2. How should West plan the play?

657. West   East
       ♠ A K 10 7 3 2   ♠ Q J 9 8
       ♡ A 7   ♡ —
       ◊ 6   ◊ A J 10 4
       ♣ A Q 7 5   ♣ 10 6 4 3 2

West is declarer at 6 ♠. North leads ♡ K. How should West plan the play?

658. West   East
       ♠ A 10 6 5 4 2   ♠ Q 8 7 3
       ♡ K 10 5 4   ♡ A Q J
       ◊ 6   ◊ A J
       ♣ A Q   ♣ 10 9 6 2

West is declarer at 6 ♠. North leads ◊ 10. How should West plan the play?

659. West   East
       ♠ None   ♠ Q 10 6 2
       ♡ A J 10 8 7   ♡ K 5 4 2
       ◊ A K Q J 4   ◊ 9 8 5
       ♣ K Q 6   ♣ A J

West is declarer at 6 ♡. North leads ♠ A. How should West plan the play?

TRUMP CONTROL

If you've played bridge for a few years you've undoubtedly had the experience of *losing control* of a trump hand. The opponents wind up with more trumps than you, and the hand "blows up in your face."

In a grim sort of way, this experience is good for you. (It happens to everybody once in a while, including the author of this book!) It teaches you to look out for trump control.

One method of keeping control of the trump suit is to lead *low* from the ace, as in Hand No. 660. Another method is to take two top cards and then abandon trumps, allowing the opponents to make whatever trumps they have left. This is shown in No. 661.

Still a third method is to give up a trump trick while dummy still has control of the enemy's suit. This plan is adopted in No. 662.

Sometimes you refuse to ruff the enemy's suit in your own hand. If you discard a sure loser, you can wait until dummy is in position to ruff the suit. This enables you to keep your own trump length.

660. West   East

    ♠ A 5 4 3 2   ♠ 8 7 6

    ♡ A K Q J 10   ♡ 6 4 2

    ♢ 4   ♢ 8 7 3 2

    ♣ 10 4   ♣ A K 5

West is declarer at 4 ♠. North leads ♢ K and continues with ♢ J. How should West plan the play?

661. West   East

    ♠ A K 10 9 8   ♠ J 5

    ♡ K 5   ♡ A Q 7 6 4

    ♢ 4   ♢ A 6 5 2

    ♣ K Q J 9 3   ♣ 10 5

West is declarer at 4 ♠. North leads ♢ Q. How should West plan the play?

662. West   East

    ♠ 6 5 2   ♠ —

    ♡ A K Q 10 7   ♡ 6 4 3

    ♢ K 9   ♢ J 10 7 5

    ♣ Q J 5   ♣ A K 10 7 6 2

West is declarer at 4 ♡. North leads ♠ K. How should West plan the play?

11. Answers to Quizzes

QUIZ No. 1

14. *Pass*. The red suits should not be counted at full value, and the hand is aceless. Bid one spade if third or fourth hand.

15. *Pass or one spade*. Changing the king of spades to the ace has made the hand a borderline case instead of a clear pass.

16. *One spade*. You now have two cards above a queen, you may count the spade and heart pictures at full value, and you have a comfortable rebid.

17. *One spade or pass*. The queens and jacks should not be counted at full value, but the hand contains an ace, a king, and a fairly good five-card suit. You would have a clear bid instead of a borderline case if the spades were headed by A-10-9.

18. *Pass*. Tend towards a pass rather than towards a bid when you have an aceless borderline hand. In third or fourth position, however, bid one spade. Open this hand in any position if *your* side has a part score; open it in first or second position if the *opponents* have a part score.

19. *One spade*. Tend towards a bid when you have a borderline hand with two aces. Compare with No. 17.

20. *One club*. Begin with clubs when you have 5-5 in the black suits. You expect to rebid twice in spades later on.

21. *One club*. The greater strength of the spades doesn't alter the bid, provided that both suits are reasonably good.

22. *One spade*. You expect to rebid in spades, ignoring the weak club suit unless partner insists on denying spade support.

23. *One club*. Treat the weak five-card spade suit like a four-card suit.

24. *One club*. Imagine that you have two four-card suits. You will show the spades comfortably at the level of one. If you

begin with one spade, you must either rebid this weak suit or risk having to bid the clubs at the level of *three*.

25. *One spade.* You expect to rebid in hearts. There is no need to treat the spades like a four-card suit, since normal bidding will give you a comfortable rebid.

26. *One spade.* You will have a comfortable rebid in diamonds over any response.

27. *One diamond or one spade.* This is a borderline case. Some experts would treat the weak spades like a four-card suit. It is probably safer to begin with the diamonds, planning to bid one spade if partner responds in hearts, but to rebid the diamonds if partner makes any other response.

28. *One diamond.* The spades are so weak that there is now no question of beginning with one spade. Compare with No. 27.

29. *One spade.* Since you have a comfortable rebid in hearts there is no reason to depart from the general rule of bidding the higher suit first.

30. *One spade.* The spades are both longer and higher, so there is no question about the proper suit to begin with.

31. *One spade.* The normal rule is to bid the longer suit first, but an opening bid of one heart would embarrass you if partner responded with one notrump or two of a minor.

32. *One heart.* You are willing to rebid two spades at your next turn since the hand is strong enough to be safe at three hearts even if partner has a weak hand.

33. *One diamond.* Over a heart response you will bid one spade. If partner responds in clubs, you will rebid in diamonds.

34. *One club.* You expect to have a comfortable rebid of one spade.

35. *One club.* You expect to have a comfortable rebid of one heart or one notrump.

36. *One diamond.* As in No. 31, you begin with the shorter suit in order to have a comfortable rebid. This is often necessary with touching suits when the hand is only moderately strong.

37. *One club*. This is the standard procedure with 4-4 in the black suits.

38. *One club*. The hand is too strong to pass, but an opening bid of one spade will leave you with no convenient rebid. The standard procedure in such cases is to open with a three-card minor suit, intending to show the major suit next if a convenient opportunity is offered.

39. *One club*. The hand is too strong to pass since the 13 points are in powerful combinations. (You might solve the problem by passing if you had 13 points in bad combinations.) You cannot afford to begin with spades and rebid in hearts, so you open with a three-card minor. You will probably have a convenient chance to rebid in one major or the other.

40. *One heart*. If partner cannot respond in spades you will abandon the suit. If partner responds in a minor, you will rebid in notrump.

41. *One diamond*. If partner responds in hearts, you will show the spade suit, such as it is. If partner responds in clubs, you will rebid in notrump.

42. *One club*. The standard course with 4-4 in the black suits.

43. *One club*. The bid is the same whether you have a strong three-card or a weak four-card club suit. In No. 41 and 42 you avoided bidding a weak suit that your partner would take seriously, but you don't mind bidding one *club* on a weak suit since a good partner will make reasonable allowance for a weak or short holding in clubs.

44. *One club*. You aren't *compelled* to have a bad hand for the opening bid of one club.

45. *One club*. With three four-card suits, begin with the suit under the singleton.

46. *One diamond*. Same reason.

47. *One heart*. In this case the suit under the singleton is rather weak, but there's no harm in treating this as a biddable suit.

48. *One spade or one heart.* If you consider the spade suit biddable (some do, some don't), treat this as another case of the suit under the singleton. If you prefer, begin with hearts on the theory that you will cheerfully give up the spade suit if partner cannot respond in it.

49. *One heart.* The spades are so weak that this hand should be treated as a 4-4 two-suiter.

QUIZ No. 2

50. *Pass.* The hand probably doesn't belong to your side, and you have no reason to encourage an opening spade lead. It might easily cost a trick.

51. *One spade.* Although you have only 10 points in high cards, the combination is good and the spade suit offers partner a very desirable opening lead. You might even bid this fourth hand, but not in first or second position.

52. *Pass.* Your spades are fine, but you have no hand.

53. *One spade.* This would not be a good bid in first or second position, but it is a fine third-hand bid. Many experts would bid it fourth hand, but they would not be astonished if they later regretted it.

54. *Pass.* You don't bid just because you have 10 points, but only if you can supply a favorable opening lead as well. In this case your partner may lead diamonds or a good suit of his own if left to his own devices, and a spade lead may conceivably cost a trick.

55. *One spade.* Since you have 12 points in high cards, the hand may belong to your side. You expect to pass partner's response.

56. *One spade.* Again the hand may belong to your side. If you are outbid and your partner leads a spade, you may be sorry, but you might be even sorrier if you passed. In any border-line situation, you will sometimes be sorry that you did one thing rather than another. Satisfaction *in the long run* is about the best that you can hope for.

57. *One spade.* You expect to pass your partner's response, so there is no need for a "prepared" bid in the three-card club suit.

58. *One club.* You expect to rebid, so you make the "prepared" bid in the short club suit.

59. *One club.* Naturally you intend to rebid with this hand, and you begin it in the normal way. It is not a law of nature that all third hand bids are weak nor that all club bids are short.

60. *One spade.* You expect to rebid in hearts. If the spades were slightly weaker, you would bid one heart and abandon the spade suit.

61. *One spade.* No question this time about wanting to rebid. Since the hand is not strong enough for a reverse, however, you must bid the shorter spade suit first.

QUIZ No. 3

62. *Pass.* You have strength in the majors but only 10 points in high cards. The hand may well belong to the opponents, and it doesn't pay to open for their benefit.

63. *One heart.* Compare with No. 55.

64. *One heart or pass.* This is a borderline case. If you do bid, show the stronger suit in the hope of indicating a favorable lead in case you are outbid. You wouldn't open this hand if your two suits were minors.

65. *One spade.* A normal bid with 12 good points and a fairly strong five-card major.

66. *Pass.* Don't open a borderline hand in fourth position with shortness in spades. You will probably be outbid.

67. *One club.* Shortness in spades doesn't worry you when you have a sound opening bid.

68. *One spade.* You expect to pass your partner's response, and the opening bid of one spade makes it more difficult for an opponent to get into the auction.

QUIZ No. 4

127. *One diamond*. It is cheaper and more informative to bid your suit than to bid 1 NT.

128. *One heart*. It is better to show a usable major than to raise a minor suit.

129. *One notrump*. J-x-x-x is hardly a *usable* suit. The response of 1 NT gives a perfect picture of your hand.

130. *Pass*. This hand obviously is too weak for any response.

131. *One spade*. You have the strength for a jump to *two* spades but you can't guarantee a strong trump suit. Hence you allow partner to make a *natural* rebid.

132. *One diamond*. A raise to three clubs would be vague and might lead to a contract of 3 NT with the hearts unstopped.

133. *Two notrump*. This hand has the perfect distribution and high card content for a 2 NT response. Don't aid and abet the enemy by showing your four-card diamond suit.

134. *Two hearts*. You have ample strength, and you can guarantee a strong trump suit. If you underbid now, you will find yourself forced to overbid or underbid later.

135. *One spade*. You certainly want to show the five-card major suit.

136. *One heart*. You are going to carry the bidding to game on this hand, and you will show your 6-5 distribution by bidding hearts first and spades later.

QUIZ No. 5

137. *Two hearts*. When your hand is worth only one response, your first duty is to raise a major suit.

138. *Pass*. Don't bid on thin air.

139. *One notrump*. The hand is barely worth a response, and your choice is between a raise and 1 NT. Because of the flat distribution you choose the notrump response.

140. *Two clubs (or two diamonds)*. Too good for two

hearts but not good enough for three. You show this by bidding a new suit; you will show support for hearts later.

141. *Two hearts.* This hand is not good enough to show the clubs and also raise hearts.

142. *One notrump.* Not nearly good enough for two clubs.

143. *Two hearts.* Your hand is worth only one response, and your first duty is to raise a major suit.

144. *Two diamonds.* You are going to bid at least twice, and you can show your distribution properly by bidding a five-card suit ahead of a four-card suit.

145. *Three clubs.* The length and solidity of your club suit plus the side ace makes the immediate jump the best way of suggesting slam possibilities.

146. *Four hearts.* This is a classic example of the immediate jump to game in a major by a player who has not previously passed.

QUIZ No. 6

147. *Two spades.* You'd rather have four trumps, but this was what you were dealt. The hand is a little too good for one notrump, but not good enough for two clubs.

148. *Three spades.* This hand is ideal for a double raise, since you have strong trumps and values in more than one of the side suits.

149. *Pass.* You might raise to two spades with favorable vulnerability (non-vulnerable against vulnerable) if you thought that the next opponent had a strong hand.

150. *One notrump.* Just enough strength to give partner a chance.

151. *Two clubs.* The hand is worth two bids. Hence you show the clubs first and plan to support spades later.

152. *One notrump.* This hand is not worth a full 10 points, and is therefore not quite worth a response at the level of two. The jack of diamonds is of doubtful value, and the doubleton in partner's suit is no asset.

153. *Two spades.* Almost worth two clubs. If the clubs were stronger or if the ♢ Q were a surer value, you would make two bids with this hand.

154. *Pass.* The safest sign-off is a pass. If the bidding is reopened, you may decide to bid the clubs; and it will then be clear that you have a good club suit in a hopeless hand. If partner suffers at one spade, his loss will be small, but if you made an immediate response of any kind, the bidding might get out of control.

155. *Two spades.* Good enough for only one response.

156. *Two clubs (or two diamonds).* Not enough for a double raise, too much for a single raise. You temporize.

157. *Three notrump.* A picture bid. Stoppers, 16 points, balanced distribution.

158. *Three clubs.* You want to start slam exploration immediately. You will try to indicate later that this forcing bid is based on spades rather than on a club suit. When making an artificial jump bid in a short suit, it is wise to prefer the minor. Moreover, on this hand you hope to discourage a club opening lead; you are not afraid of a heart lead.

QUIZ No. 7

159. *Pass.* Any response is likely to stir partner to a jump rebid. There is no need for action to keep the opponents out; they have both passed originally.

160. *Two spades.* If you bid two clubs, partner is allowed to pass. Two spades is an underbid, but is still your best action.

161. *Three spades.* A slight overbid, but the best available action. As a passed hand, you must usually choose between an underbid and an overbid when you have good support for partner's major suit.

162. *Three spades.* If partner passes (allowable, since you have passed originally), you should be safe at three spades.

163. *Four spades.* This hand should be enough to produce

game even if partner has opened a doubtful hand. A raise to three spades might be passed.

164. *Two clubs.* The hand is a near-maximum pass, but it would be foolish to bid three clubs. If partner has a doubtful hand, why should you force him? If he has a sound hand, he will bid voluntarily.

165. *Three clubs.* This shows a maximum pass and a fit. You intend to get to four spades, and you give some information on the way just in case partner has a good hand and wants to bid a slam.

QUIZ No. 8

193. *One notrump.* Show that you have a balanced minimum opening bid.

194. *Two hearts.* You had expected to bid the spades next, but your hand is not worth *three* bids.

195. *One spade.* Two hearts would be an underbid and three hearts an overbid with only three trumps. You compromise by showing the spades, intending to raise hearts later.

196. *Three hearts.* This hand is clearly worth the double raise.

197. *One notrump.* The important story is that you have a balanced minimum bid. The weak spade suit is hardly worth thinking about.

198. *Four hearts.* Game should be easy even if partner has a very weak hand.

199. *Two notrump.* A "reverse" of two diamonds would show strength, but the jump in notrump gives a better picture of your hand, without helping the opponents.

200. *Two spades.* Too strong for a raise to four hearts. The forcing bid in a new suit, followed by strong heart support, will suggest the slam possibilities to partner much more vividly. If partner raises spades, you can afford to get higher.

201. *One spade.* You may never get another convenient chance to bid the spades.

202. *Two clubs*. The spades are hardly worth showing. The strength of the club suit is the important story in this hand.

203. *Two spades*. A rebid of one spade would not be forcing. You are willing to be in game opposite any hand that was strong enough for just one response.

204. *Three notrump*. You cannot settle for less than game, and no forcing bid tells your story.

QUIZ No. 9

205. *Three hearts*. A forcing rebid, since partner has shown strength.

206. *Three clubs*. The hand is strong enough for a rebid at the level of three.

207. *Two hearts*. The hand is not strong enough for a rebid at the level of three.

208. *Three diamonds*. The hearts are, of course, highly rebiddable, but with your general strength and the good diamond fit you must make the more encouraging rebid.

209. *Two notrump*. This rebid shows a balanced hand of about 13 to 15 points, with a stopper in at least one of the unbid suits.

210. *Four hearts*. You surely want to play at game after partner's strength-showing response. This kind of rebid shows a completely independent suit.

211. *Three hearts*. The heart suit itself is not good enough for a jump to four. Nevertheless, you will probably wind up in four hearts.

QUIZ No. 10

212. *Pass*. Game is out of the question and there is no reason to rebid the hearts with this balanced distribution.

213. *Two clubs*. Not good enough for three clubs and not the hand for a raise in notrump despite the fact that each of the doubletons is headed by the queen.

214. *Three spades*. You want to make sure of reaching a

game. *Two spades is not a forcing bid* nor would three hearts be.

215. *Three hearts.* You can invite partner to go to game but you cannot insist on it. Two diamonds would be too weak a bid.

216. *Two hearts.* You have too many obvious losers to make a game try. If partner has a maximum notrump he can bid again.

QUIZ No. 11

217. *Three hearts.* This is forcing. You are asking partner to choose the game contract—four hearts or three notrump.

218. *Three diamonds.* You will not settle for less than a small slam. If partner shows a great liking for diamonds, you will think about a grand slam.

219. *Four notrump.* Partner will bid a slam if he has maximum values. Otherwise he will pass at a safe contract.

220. *Three spades.* Game may be safer in one of the majors. Give partner the choice.

221. *Three notrump.* With your balanced minimum and with strength in every suit you should not prefer four hearts to three notrump.

QUIZ No. 12

222. *Four clubs.* You have a remarkably good club fit and should establish that at once.

223. *Three hearts.* Another example of a natural bid in response to partner's force.

224. *Three spades.* You are going to bid much higher, but there is no need to leap immediately. Establish the strength of your spade suit first, and your subsequent bids will easily fall into line.

225. *Four spades.* It can only help partner to learn at once that your spades are independent.

226. *Three notrump.* The spades are theoretically rebid-

dable, but the important story here is that you have a balanced minimum bid.

QUIZ No. 13

227. *Pass.* Not enough over a minimum to make game seem likely after partner can bid only two spades.

228. *Four spades.* You want to play game and you're not interested in slam. Showing the side suit may help the opponents, but it won't help you.

229. *Three spades.* If partner has maximum values, you want him to bid game. You should be safe at three spades even if he has a minimum.

230. *Three diamonds.* There is no need to jump, since this bid is forcing. If partner's natural response is encouraging (such as four diamonds, four clubs, or a jump to four spades) you will bid a slam.

231. *Three hearts.* There may be a better play for game in hearts than in spades.

QUIZ No. 14

232. *Four hearts.* Three spades would be a slam try, and you will be happy enough to make game.

233. *Four clubs.* You will surely bid a slam eventually. If partner has a fit for clubs, you will think about a grand slam.

234. *Four clubs.* It would not be wrong to bid four hearts. An aggressive player would bid four clubs and then leave the rest to partner. You should be safe at five hearts even if nothing comes of your one mild slam try.

235. *Four hearts.* It would be wrong to try notrump with the doubleton diamond, just because you have a minimum hand.

236. *Three notrump.* Here you have five hearts but kings in the other three suits. If partner passes three notrump the 9-trick game should be easier.

QUIZ No. 15

239. *Pass.* Since partner has at most 15 points, there is no game in this hand.

240. *Two notrump.* Your 11 points will be enough for game if partner has 15 points or even a good 14 points.

241. *Two diamonds.* This bid suggests a better part score contract.

242. *Three notrump.* Easier than game at diamonds.

243. *Pass.* Let sleeping dogs lie. If one notrump is doubled, however, you will bid the clubs.

244. *Two hearts.* Safer than one notrump. If partner unexpectedly raises hearts, you will go on to game.

245. *Three hearts.* The hand will probably produce a game. If partner goes to three notrump, you will pass.

246. *Four hearts.* Since you don't intend to pass three notrump, you might just as well go to four hearts at once.

247. *Three clubs.* Two clubs would not be forcing, and you certainly want to play for game somewhere.

248. *Two spades.* The reverse by responding hand is forcing.

QUIZ No. 16

249. *Four spades.* There should be a good play for game.

250. *Three spades.* If partner has maximum value, you should have a good play for game.

251. *Two notrump.* With 11 points in high cards, you want to make a second response.

252. *Three notrump.* With 15 points opposite an opening bid, you must insist on getting to game. Partner may choose between spades and notrump.

253. *Pass.* Since partner has about 16 points at most, game must be out of the question.

QUIZ No. 17

254. *Three notrump.* Partner should have about 19 points, and your 7 points should give him a play for game.

255. *Three notrump.* You have no good reason to think that spades will be better than notrump.

256. *Three spades.* This is forcing. You will try for a slam later, but will best know what to do after finding out whether or not partner can raise spades.

257. *Three clubs.* This is an exploratory bid to see whether the hand should play at spades or notrump. If your partner bids three spades you will go to game there. If partner bids three notrump you will pass.

258. *Pass.* Partner's bid is not forcing, and you cannot find another bid.

QUIZ No. 18

259. *Three notrump.* Your choice is between a jump to three spades and a jump to three notrump. The balanced distribution is an argument for the jump in notrump.

260. *Three spades.* You are too strong for two spades but don't want to insist on a spade contract by bidding four spades. If over three spades partner bids three notrump, that's where the hand should play.

261. *Four spades.* Since you don't intend to pass three notrump, you bid the game that you do favor.

262. *Three hearts.* You have better than a mere preference bid of two hearts. The diamond fit should help him.

263. *Pass.* Your first response was doubtful, but a second response would be criminal.

264. *Three diamonds.* You cannot bid notrump without a proper stopper in the unbid suit. Since you do want to make a second response with your 11 points, the diamond raise is a must.

265. *Two hearts.* You can afford to give your partner another chance. If he goes on to game after this simple preference, you can stand it.

266. *Four hearts*. The possibilities are three spades, three hearts, and four hearts. If you jump in spades, you will be unable to show the heart strength except by going past game. Three hearts is a flagrant underbid. The objections to four hearts are mildest.

267. *Pass*. With hands of 6 to 9 points you make only one voluntary response.

268. *Three clubs*. You know that you want to reach game, but you don't know *which* game. If partner bids three diamonds you will bid three hearts; if he bids three hearts, you will bid four hearts. And if he bids three notrump, that is his spot.

QUIZ No. 19

269. *Pass*. The diamond fit shouldn't excite you. With hands of 6 to 9 points you make only one voluntary response.

270. *Three diamonds*. With 10 points in high cards you can afford a second voluntary response. The raise in diamonds describes your values better than a rebid of two notrump.

271. *Two notrump*. Once again, you can afford a second response with 10 points in high cards. Since your strength is in the unbid suits, you suggest notrump.

272. *Two spades*. You would not make a second response with only 7 points, but a *preference* is not really a bid. Compare with Hand No. 265, and contrast with No. 263.

QUIZ No. 20

273. *Three hearts*. Since you have already shown strength by bidding two clubs, a simple raise will now do justice to your hand. You have already promised 10 points, which is very nearly all you have.

274. *Four hearts*. Since you have considerably more than your first response promised, you must make a second strong bid.

275. *Two spades*. This unusual bid will steer partner into notrump if he can take care of diamonds. If he rebids the hearts

again, you will raise to game. It is very unlikely that partner can raise spades since he has had two chances to bid the suit himself.

QUIZ No. 21

276. *Three hearts*. Partner should have about 18 points for his reverse, and your hand may well be good enough to provide a play for game.

277. *Pass*. Partner's reverse, although a strong bid, is not a force. You cannot support either red suit, nor can you bid notrump with the spades wide open. You have been asked for a preference, and you prefer hearts.

278. *Three diamonds*. Partner has more diamonds than hearts, and has asked you to choose between his suits.

279. *Two notrump*. With good stoppers in both of the unbid suits you suggest game in notrump.

280. *Two spades*. You will bid four hearts next. Partner knows that you don't have biddable spades (since you failed to bid them the first time) and will therefore realize that you are making a cue-bid and mildly suggesting a slam.

QUIZ No. 22

309. *One notrump*. A "book" example of a minimum notrump.

310. *Two notrump*. Just the right strength and texture.

311. *One notrump*. Only 15 points but the two tens and the nine should allow you this bit of license.

312. *One notrump*. A much more descriptive bid than one club despite the five-card club suit.

313. *One club*. Too strong for 1 NT but not strong enough for 2 NT.

314. *Two diamonds*. The *shape* is wrong for an opening bid of 3 NT. It would be easy to miss a slam if you failed to open with two in your best suit.

315. *One notrump*. The weak doubleton in diamonds is,

of course, a flaw, but the hand is otherwise ideal for notrump. There are drawbacks to all other opening bids. Some experts would, however, open with one spade, one heart, or one club.

316. *Three no trump.* Slightly too strong for 2 NT because of the length in diamonds.

317. *One notrump.* A 17-point maximum notrump.

QUIZ No. 23

318. *Pass.* Too weak for even the weakness response of two spades. Furthermore, you cannot be sure that two spades will be any easier to make than one notrump.

319. *Four spades.* Don't beat about the bush when you know exactly where you want to play the hand.

320. *Two hearts.* Because of the unbalanced distribution two hearts should be safer than one notrump.

321. *Two clubs.* A Stayman response. If partner bids two spades, you will raise to four spades. If he bids anything else, you will bid three notrump.

322. *Two clubs.* If partner bids two spades you will raise to four spades. If he bids anything else, you will go to 3 NT, gambling on the clubs to come in.

323. *Three notrump.* Don't go out of your way to look for game in a major when your distribution is 4-3-3-3.

324. *Three spades.* You want to give your partner a choice of game in spades or notrump. If his rebid is three notrump you will pass. Otherwise, you will wind up at four spades.

325. *Two clubs.* You don't know whether the hand should play in notrump or in hearts; at a part score, or at game. A response of two hearts would be an underbid, and three hearts would be an overbid.

You first bid two clubs. If partner bids two hearts, you raise. If he bids two diamonds, you will bid two hearts. If North rebids two notrump, showing a maximum, you bid three hearts and thus give him a choice between game in hearts and notrump. If partner's rebid is two spades, you will then conceal the hearts and bid two notrump.

326. *Two clubs.* The hand is too good for two hearts but not good enough for three hearts. Bid two clubs, and then bid minimums in hearts over whatever partner does.

QUIZ No. 24

327. *Three notrump.* Ample strength to raise from 2 NT to game.

328. *Pass.* Three points is not enough for a raise.

329. *Three diamonds.* You will next bid four notrump, thus inviting a slam and indicating that your long diamond suit may help produce twelve tricks.

330. *Three clubs.* If partner can respond three hearts, game will be safer there; otherwise, the final contract will be three notrump.

331. *Four notrump.* With no five-card suit, slam is not too likely unless partner has a maximum. The double notrump raise ideally portrays your hand and permits of a pass by partner at a safe level if he has a minimum. This four notrump bid is not Blackwood.

QUIZ No. 25

332. *Two diamonds.* A minimum notrump. The four-card spade suit is too weak to show.

333. *Two notrump.* A maximum notrump and no biddable major.

334. *Two spades.* With both majors, show spades first.

335. *Two spades.* Whether maximum or minimum, the rebid is the same.

336. *Two hearts.* Shows biddable hearts; denies biddable spades.

QUIZ No. 26

337. *Two notrump*. North is allowed to pass with a minimum notrump.

338. *Three notrump*. There should be a good play for three notrump even opposite a bare 16 points.

339. *Two spades*. Forcing for one round. You will make sure of reaching game in spades or notrump.

340. *Three notrump*. You were hoping for a two-heart rebid by your partner, but since that was not to be you have to risk game in notrump.

341. *Three clubs*. A sign-off showing partner that your first bid was not intended as Stayman. Three clubs is where the hand should play. (Some experts show this by jumping to three clubs at the first turn.)

QUIZ No. 27

342. *Three diamonds*. Partner has a maximum notrump and no biddable major. Slam in one of the minors is highly likely. Since three diamonds is a forcing bid you can go slowly and find out which is the fitting minor suit.

343. *Three hearts*. Partner cannot pass this and you want to give him the choice between game in hearts and notrump.

344. *Three notrump*. We have only 8 points, but partner has shown a maximum. There should be a play for game.

345. *Three notrump*. Partner will pass three clubs. Since he has a maximum notrump there should be a good play for game since it is odds-on that the club suit can be brought in.

QUIZ No. 28

346. *Four hearts*. Three hearts would not be forcing and would be a decided underbid.

347. *Three hearts*. Partner may pass if he has a minimum notrump.

348. *Two notrump*. Partner may pass if he has a minimum notrump.

349. *Two spades*. A force for one round. If partner raises, you will bid four spades; otherwise, three notrump.

350. *Three notrump*. This should be as good as four spades, perhaps better. You might be worried with a weak doubleton, but with not K-x.

QUIZ No. 29

374. *Three hearts*. A typical hand for this shutout bid.

375. *Three hearts*. A 7-card suit is preferred, but the 4-card side suit will probably serve the same purpose.

376. *Pass*. Do not make a shutout bid in first or second position when you hold an ace. In third position you would bid three hearts.

377. *Pass*. Avoid making a shutout bid in a minor suit when you have support for one or both of the majors.

378. *Pass*. It is too dangerous to bid three hearts against red-blooded opponents. Make a shutout bid only when playing against children or very old ladies.

379. *Four hearts*. Go all the way when you can. An 8-card suit will protect you from disaster.

380. *Pass or one heart*. Do not make a shutout bid on a hand with full top command of a long suit. (You would bid three hearts with a fully informed partner if you were vulnerable and the opponents were not.)

QUIZ No. 30

381. *Pass*. Not good enough for a vulnerable bid of three hearts.

382. *Three hearts*. This hand may well play two tricks better than No. 381.

383. *Four hearts*. Bid a freakish hand to the hilt. It would be criminal to bid only three and bid more later.

384. *Pass.* Too much side strength for a shutout bid in first or second position. In third position, however, you would bid three hearts.

385. *Three diamonds.* A side queen needn't stop you from making a shutout bid in first or second position.

QUIZ No. 31

386. *Pass.* Game is unlikely. Any bid will simply get you overboard.

387. *Four hearts.* If the hand fits, there will be a reasonable play for game. Even if the fit is poor, no great harm should result.

388. *Four hearts.* The opponents should have a slam, but you may talk them out of it if their strength is evenly divided. Each opponent may credit you with the missing strength, and each may therefore be afraid to come in.

389. *Pass.* The opponents should have four aces and a king, since your partner guarantees that he does not have top strength when he opens with three. If you pass quickly and casually, the opponents may get into trouble.

390. *Four hearts.* There should be a good play for this even if partner has the typical hand of seven hearts to K-Q-J. Don't even dream of slam; he may have trouble enough making game.

QUIZ No. 32

391. *Pass.* You were badly overboard at *three* hearts.

392. *Pass.* Partner can probably make 9 or 10 tricks at hearts, but the opponents can probably make a slam at spades or diamonds. The surest way to get them to slam is to push them into it! If you pass, they may stop at game.

393. *Six hearts!* You may even make this if partner is void of spades. The opponents probably have a slam in diamonds, and your bid is intended to keep them out of it at small cost. If they go to slam in spades, you may give them an interesting time!

394. *Pass.* If the enemy stay in spades you will be pleased.

Don't dream of scaring them away from the only contract you can defeat.

395. *Double*. You are ready to double everything from here on. You wouldn't double unless you could handle any possible rescue.

QUIZ No. 33

396. *Pass*. The hand is a sound bid of *one* spade, not three.

397. *Three spades*. You can come reasonably close to this contract with practically no help at all from partner.

398. *Double*. Spades are best, but you are ready to support the other suits if necessary. If partner has to pass for penalties you will shed no tears.

399. *Four spades*. You should make this contract if partner has any ace or the king in either of your long suits. You should not ask him to bid game on such small holdings.

400. *Pass*. If you double, partner will bid; and you may wind up with a minus score. If you pass, you will almost surely get a substantial plus.

401. *Three notrump*. Not guaranteed, since North may have a long spade or club suit and a good hand. A good shot, nevertheless.

402. *Three notrump*. Practically guaranteed.

QUIZ No. 34

403. *Three hearts*. Keep your fingers crossed. This hand may turn out badly.

404. *Pass*. You should take two or three tricks on defense, and partner should take about four. You have no safe spot of your own.

405. *Four hearts*. Make it clear that you don't have the miseries, as in Hand No. 403. Take partner off the anxious seat.

406. *Four diamonds*. This cue bid asks partner to choose the suit. You will be pleased with game in either major.

407. *Four diamonds*. This time you really mean the cue bid. When partner names his suit, you will raise right to slam.

QUIZ No. 35

439. *Four spades*. With balanced distribution, you need an ace more than an opening bid to make a slam try.

440. *Four spades*. With unbalanced distribution, you need a king more than a minimum opening bid in order to make a slam try. You have the minimum values for your opening bid.

441. *Four hearts*. Even if the king of diamonds were a small card, you would still have a sound opening bid. Hence you are entitled to make a slam try.

442. *Four diamonds*. Even if the ace of diamonds were a small card, you would still have a sound opening bid. Hence you are justified in making a slam try. It would be foolish to use the Blackwood Convention, since you would not know how to proceed after discovering how many aces your partner holds.

443. *Four hearts*. You have the equivalent of an ace more than a mere opening bid, and you are therefore justified in making a slam try. Make your cue bid in the suit in which you hold the ace.

444. *Four spades*. You cannot afford to make a slam try, and there is no advantage in telling your partner about the hearts. Play the hand safely at game, and conceal your long side suit from the enemy.

445. *Four hearts*. You can afford to make this slam try since you would have opened the bidding even with two small diamonds instead of your actual holding. Slam is unlikely unless partner can show considerable enthusiasm.

446. *Four notrump*. A good hand for the Blackwood Convention. If partner shows only one ace, you will stop at six spades. If he shows two aces, you will take your chances on a grand slam.

447. *Four notrump*. You cannot make a cue bid, for lack of aces. The Blackwood Convention should, however, see you

through. If partner shows two aces, you will stop at six spades. If he shows three aces, you will go to the grand slam in spades.

448. *Four diamonds.* If partner can make a cue bid in hearts, you will consider a grand slam. You do not use the Blackwood Convention, since you are not at all interested in the number of aces partner holds but *which* particular ace he holds.

QUIZ No. 36

449. *Four spades.* You have minimum values for the double raise and no value for a slam. You must sign off.

450. *Four spades.* You have minimum values for your double raise and should avoid encouraging your partner with a cue bid in hearts.

451. *Four hearts.* You can afford to encourage partner with a return cue bid in hearts because you have excellent values for your double raise.

452. *Four spades.* You cannot afford to show the excellent heart suit because such a bid would show the ace rather than just a suit. Since you have minimum values for your double raise, you are not interested in encouraging your partner's slam ambitions.

453. *Five spades.* The jump bid indicates your interest in slam, and the failure to make a cue bid indicates that you have no aces. Partner should have no trouble in working out the kind of hand you must hold.

454. *Five clubs.* You expect to reach six spades, but there is no harm in showing your ace on the way.

455. *Four notrump.* A cue bid of four hearts might not tell your partner enough. You can settle the future of this hand by using the Blackwood Convention. If partner shows three aces, you will bid a grand slam. If he shows only two aces, you will stop at six spades.

456. *Six spades.* You have no ace to show, and the Blackwood Convention is not particularly useful when you have a void suit. The best bet is to jump right to slam. If a club is opened,

South should make the slam without any trouble. He will probably have a fine play for the slam even if a heart is opened.

QUIZ No. 37

457. *Four spades.* You could barely afford the slam try of four diamonds, and you must therefore leave the next move up to partner.

458. *Five spades.* The jump in this situation invites partner to bid the slam if he can take care of the first or second trick in the unbid suit.

459. *Five diamonds.* If North can repeat his cue bid in hearts, you will try for a grand slam in spades. Otherwise, you may be satisfied with a small slam.

460. *Five spades.* As in the case of Hand No. 458, you are inviting your partner to bid a slam if he can take care of the first or second trick in the unbid suit.

461. *Six spades.* You are not quite strong enough to try for a grand slam, as in Hand No. 459. The fit is, however, good enough to justify your jump to slam.

QUIZ No. 38

462. *Three hearts.* Avoid bidding the other suit when you have a perfectly normal rebid in your first suit. You don't want to encourage slam ambitions when you suspect that the hand is a misfit.

463. *Three diamonds.* Since the hand is not a misfit, there is no harm in showing your good side suit.

464. *Three diamonds.* You expect to reach a slam, but you are not sure of the suit. Normal patient bidding will tell you in time.

465. *Three notrump.* This indicates a minimum opening bid with balanced distribution.

466. *Three diamonds.* You tend to make the slightly more encouraging rebid because of the fit with partner's clubs.

467. *Three diamonds*. You can well afford to encourage partner since you have two aces and a reasonable fit for his suit.

468. *Four clubs*. You are glad to show partner the excellent fit for his suit.

469. *Three hearts*. The big news about this hand is the fact that the hearts are strong and rebiddable.

470. *Four hearts*. This shows an absolutely solid suit. This information may enable partner to pick the final contract at his next turn.

471. *Three hearts*. You intend to use the Blackwood Convention, and might do so at this turn without being criticized. There is no harm, however, in finding out what else partner can say before you jump to four notrump.

QUIZ No. 39

472. *Three diamonds*. You will next raise the spades, thus showing a strong hand with excellent spade support and a singleton in the unbid suit.

473. *Four spades*. This strong bid urges partner to try for a slam, but your failure to make a forcing rebid in a new suit hints that you do not have a singleton or void suit to tell him about.

474. *Three diamonds or four notrump*. This is a borderline case. If you are optimistic, use the Blackwood Convention to find out how many aces partner holds. If he has one ace, you intend to bid six spades; if he has two aces, you will consider a grand slam. If you are less optimistic, you will bid three diamonds at this turn and jump to five spades at your next turn. This allows partner to wriggle out if he has made his first response with a very poor hand.

475. *Six spades*. If you bid this hand scientifically, a diamond opening lead may give your partner some trouble. If you jump all the way to slam, however, your partner may get a more favorable opening lead. There is no great virtue in bidding this

hand scientifically, since you are not likely to bid a grand slam anyway.

QUIZ No. 40

476. *Six spades*. Partner must have exactly the kind of hand that will make slam a laydown.

477. *Pass*. You will probably lose a spade and either a heart or a club. The diamond strength is a duplication of values, since South has advertised a singleton. A losing heart is likewise not out of the question.

478. *Bid six spades*. You have duplication of strength in diamonds, but the rest of the hand is good enough for the slam. You might make the same bid even if your king of diamonds were changed to a small card.

479. *Four notrump*. If partner shows three aces, you expect to bid five notrump to check on his kings. You are considering a grand slam in spades, and your partner will have to give you very discouraging responses to stop you from reaching this contract.

QUIZ No. 41
(Neither side is vulnerable)

520. *Double*. This is a minimum, but you can stand any suit that partner responds in, even though it is at the level of two. Your distribution makes up for your meager 11 points.

521. *Pass*. Too shaky for an overcall at the two level, even not vulnerable. If the opening bid were one club, you would bid one heart.

522. *Double*. You can afford to take some action, but you don't want to put all your eggs in one basket. A double gives you the best chance to reach a safe contract in any of the three unbid suits.

523. *Two diamonds*. The strong six-card suit is worth an overcall, mostly for the purpose of indicating a lead.

524. *Double*. You will bid hearts later, thus promising a very good hand.

525. *Pass.* Any action is likely to get you on the hook and the opponents off. Make it a habit to pass quickly and casually when you are *loaded* with the enemy's suit.

526. *Two diamonds.* You are tempted to pass because of the strength in spades, but the odds are that the enemy will find a good spot in hearts or clubs. You must bid the diamonds while it is still easy to do so.

527. *Double.* Your strength in the unbid major calls for a double.

528. *One notrump.* Do not double for a takeout when you are short in the unbid major. This overcall promises much the same as an opening bid of one notrump.

529. *Two diamonds.* If partner cannot act voluntarily, the hand has no future. A takeout double would promise more length in hearts.

530. *Two spades.* This demands game and asks partner to choose the suit.

531. *Double.* You will bid hearts later, thus promising a very good hand.

QUIZ No. 42

(Both sides are vulnerable)

520. *Pass.* You cannot risk the double when vulnerable.

521. *Pass.* Vulnerable, this hand is not worth a heart overcall even at the one level.

522. *Pass.* Too weak for vulnerable action. If the opponents have a part score, you might risk coming in. A takeout double would then be preferred to a heart overcall.

523. *Pass.* Only a part-score situation would justify a vulnerable overcall at the two level with this hand.

524. *Double.* Vulnerability affects your action only when you have a weak hand.

525. *Pass.* Playing to trap vulnerable opponents is even more inviting than when they were not vulnerable.

526. *Pass or two diamonds.* A borderline case. Either the

trap pass or the overcall may produce a good result. Trap against a wild bidder; overcall against a conservative bidder.

527. *Double*. Again, vulnerability doesn't change your action when you have a strong hand.

528. *One notrump*. Again, the vulnerability does not change things.

529. *Two diamonds*. This hand just barely makes the grade for a vulnerable overcall at the two level.

530. *Two spades*. The vulnerability does not change your bid.

531. *Double*. Again, the vulnerability does not change your bid.

QUIZ No. 43
(Only your side is vulnerable)

520. *Pass*. Still more dangerous to come in when you are vulnerable and the opponents are not.

521. *Pass*.

522. *Pass*.

523. *Pass*.

524. *Double*.

525. *Pass or one notrump*. If the opening bidder is a sound player, you will trust his bid and pass. If he is an "operator," you may have to come in to prevent the enemy from talking you out of a game. In most games the pass is recommended.

526. *Two diamonds*. You stand to gain less from trapping and more from bidding than in the both-vulnerable case.

527. *Double*.

528. *One notrump*.

529. *Two diamonds*.

530. *Two spades*.

531. *Double*.

QUIZ No. 44

(Only the opponents vulnerable)

520. *Double.* Not vulnerable, you can afford to compete.

521. *Pass or two hearts.* The favorable vulnerability may tempt you. You may risk this doubtful overcall at the two level for lead-directing purposes and general nuisance value.

522. *Double.*

523. *Three diamonds.* The pre-emptive overcall may interfere with the bidding of the vulnerable opponents.

524. *Double.*

525. *Pass.* The trap pass is desirable with this vulnerability.

526. *Pass.* The trap pass is better with this vulnerability.

527. *Double.* Your strength in the other major makes a trap pass undesirable even though they are vulnerable and you are not.

528. *Pass.* The trap pass will produce better results in the long run than direct action.

529. *Two diamonds.*

530. *Two spades.* It would be pointless to try to trap when you are void in the enemy's suit.

531. *Double.*

QUIZ No. 45

532. *One spade.* Don't think of passing the double for penalties with a diamond holding as weak as this. Don't worry about the weakness of your spade suit. Your partner has taken the responsibility.

533. *One heart.* The four-card major should be preferred to the five-card minor.

534. *One spade.* Not quite good enough for a jump.

535. *Four hearts.* Even partner's weakest double of one diamond should give you a play for game in hearts.

536. *Two spades.* Easily enough for the jump response.

537. *Two diamonds.* The forcing response. Now you have time to explore all roads to game.

538. *One notrump.* This response shows at least one stopper in the enemy's suit and a smattering of strength.

539. *One heart.* The pass is out of the question. With hopeless hands of this sort bid the cheapest three-card suit.

QUIZ No. 46

540. *Pass.* Game is out of the question when partner fails to make a jump response.

541. *Pass.* Again, there is no game if partner can make only a minimum response.

542. *Three hearts.* Game in hearts seems very likely, and game in spades will be a good bet if partner can rebid. This jump is not 100 per cent forcing since you failed to bid two diamonds over the opening bid of one diamond. Nevertheless, partner is expected to bid except with a completely barren hand.

543. *Two hearts.* This sequence promises a very good hand and urges partner to bid.

544. *Three spades.* Partner is expected to go on with as little as a king or so. If he has less than this, you will be glad you stopped at three.

QUIZ No. 47

577. *Pass.* You would keep the bidding open for partner with one notrump had East not overcalled. East's bid relieves you of this duty.

578. *One spade.* It is true that East's overcall relieves you of the necessity of coming in on doubtful hands. However, you have a decent five-card suit, and your free bid can be made at the level of one. It is much better to make this bid now at the low level than to guess whether or not to come in later.

579. *Pass.* The temptation to make a business double of the opposing overcall is great but should be avoided. You cannot stand any rescue of the heart double that either *your partner or your opponents may make.* If your partner, when it comes around

to him, should make a takeout double of the one-heart contract, you will then pass for penalties and partner will know where he stands.

580. *One notrump.* This shows a fairly good hand and a probable double heart stopper. If you bid two clubs you will feel impelled to make a second bid later to show the heart stoppers, and this would clearly be overbidding your strength.

581. *Two diamonds.* The free raise to two diamonds shows the strength of this hand. If there is a game in spades, partner will be able to bid two spades over two diamonds. Had there been no overcall, you would have responded with *one* spade.

QUIZ No. 48

582. *Pass.* You have a minimum opening bid and should not take any further action even to compete for the part score.

583. *Three spades.* Your distribution justifies this rebid. If your partner takes you seriously and goes on to game there should be a play for it.

584. *Four spades.* After your partner's free raise you want to play for game with this hand. Don't leave it up to partner to bid what you can bid all by yourself.

585. *Four clubs.* There is some chance for a slam after partner's free raise to two spades.

586. *Four notrump.* After partner's free raise you are willing to get at least to the five level. If partner has two aces, and he very easily might have, you want to be at six.

QUIZ No. 49

587. *Pass.* You have raised freely on the first round and have very little over your free raise.

588. *Four spades.* You had a maximum raise to two spades. Even allowing partner some leeway for having bid three spades competitively, there should be a good play for game.

QUIZ No. 50

589. *Pass.* Clearly not enough to bid over the intervening notrump overcall.

590. *Double.* If your partner has a good hand the opponents are in trouble.

591. *Double.* If East stays in one notrump doubled, you will lead the king of spades and should collect a fat profit. If East runs out of notrump, you will then bid your spades; and it will be clear that you have a good hand.

592. *Two hearts.* Not a strong bid since you failed to double one notrump.

593. *Double.* You must double first to show your strength.

QUIZ No. 51

594. *Pass.* Not strong enough to push the bidding to a high level.

595. *Two hearts.* You still cannot afford to bid the spades but you can afford to raise hearts.

596. *Two spades.* You will probably have to push to game in spades or hearts. Show the spades first and the heart support later.

597. *Double.* Two diamonds would be an awkward bid with this poor suit and two notrump would be an overbid. If partner can stand your double of two clubs you should set the opponents, perhaps substantially.

598. *Three diamonds.* Show the long suit first and save the cue bid in clubs for later. You may want an absolutely forcing bid (such as five clubs) after game has been reached.

599. *Two hearts.* Strong enough for a free raise over the intervening overcall.

600. *Pass.* Not strong enough for a free raise.

601. *Three hearts.* Don't rely on a mere free raise when you have the values for a double raise.

QUIZ No. 52

602. *Three hearts.* If you bid three diamonds you may play it there and go down miserably, with three or four hearts a lay-down. If partner's two-heart overcall had been vulnerable, you would have been good enough to jump to four hearts.

603. *Three hearts.* Game is unlikely, since partner has made a simple overcall rather than a takeout double. You raise, nevertheless, for pre-emptive or competitive reasons.

604. *Two spades.* There may be a slam in this hand, particularly if the overcall is vulnerable. Two spades is the only forcing bid available to you. After partner rebids, if you then go to four hearts he will know you are interested in slam. If his rebid is a strong one, you may go it alone.

605. *Pass.* Don't try to rescue on so poor a hand and so weak a suit. You have not even been doubled at two hearts. If North subsequently doubles and South leaves it in, you can then reconsider the matter.

606. *Three hearts.* If your partner's overcall is vulnerable, it is absolutely clear-cut that some action must be taken. The doubleton queen is certainly adequate trump support opposite a vulnerable overcall at the two level. With only a single spade stopper, the heart raise is preferable to two notrump, and the barren aces should be more valuable at suit play. The raise to three hearts is the correct bid even when your side is not vulnerable, although then it would not be quite as craven to pass.

QUIZ No. 53

607. *Redouble.* First show your strength by way of the redouble. Later you will clarify your bid.

608. *Pass.* With a balanced hand and only 6 points, there is no need to take any action.

609. *One spade.* You can well afford to bid now, but it might be expensive to bid at your next turn if you passed now.

610. *One notrump.* This bid shows about 9 scattered points —not enough for a redouble, but enough to be worth describing.

611. *Redouble.* You will surely bid game in hearts, but you can afford to redouble on the way. There may even be a slam in this hand.

612. *Three hearts.* A pre-emptive double raise over an intervening double. This hand would be worth only two hearts had East not doubled. Now you can afford to bid three and partner will not take you too seriously since you did not redouble.

613. *Pass.* Do not rescue unless you are sure that your suit is better than your partner's.

614. *Three diamonds.* The jump takeout over an intervening double is played as a one-round force by some and as only a strong urge by others. Either way you play it, it is correct on this hand. You cannot afford to redouble with the singleton heart and not too much in high cards, but you are clearly too good for a measly two diamond bid over the double.

615. *Two diamonds.* You can afford to bid now, but may not be able to afford a bid later.

616. *Redouble.* The heart fit makes this hand just about strong enough to redouble.

QUIZ No. 54

617. *One notrump.* Only 14 points, but the 4-3-3-3 distribution makes this the ideal call with your side 60 on score. Partner now knows he can compete in any suit he may have.

618. *Two spades.* An opening two-bid must be kept open at least once, even with 60. It is naive to open with only one spade on a huge hand such as this just because you feel fairly certain your partner will not pass you out with 60. Even if partner does keep it open you will never be able to show your strength adequately. By opening with two spades you can suggest slam by a simple non-jump bid in hearts on the next round and partner will know whether or not to take you any higher.

619. *Two notrump.* This would normally be worth three

notrump, but since two notrump is a bid past game it serves well enough as a slam suggestion.

620. *One spade.* You are ready to pass any response. If your hand were a little stronger and you had the intention of making a second bid competitively all by yourself, you would then prefer the club opening.

621. *One notrump.* Even though this hand is not 4-3-3-3 in pattern it is still an ideal notrump with 60 on score. One diamond or one club would make things too easy for the opponents. Your 14 points plus two tens should provide safety.

QUIZ No. 55

622. *One heart.* Not good enough for an opening bid normally. In this case you may want to show both suits and must begin while it is still cheap to bid.

623. *One notrump.* Here the balanced notrump is directed against the opponents' score. It may shut them out; and if they do come in, the notrump bid will enable your partner to help push them up.

QUIZ No. 56

624. *Two hearts.* If pushed, you can then bid three diamonds and thus give partner his choice at the level of three. If you bid the diamonds first and later have to bid three hearts, you will lose the chance to play the hand at three diamonds.

625. *Two clubs.* The two-over-one bid is not forcing with the part score. You can therefore afford to respond naturally in your long suit.

626. *Three hearts.* The bid over game is a mild slam suggestion.

627. *One spade.* You will raise to three hearts next, thus showing your mild slam ambitions and your spade strength at the same time.

628. *One notrump.* This underbid may well trap the enemy into a competitive bid. If so, you will double for penalties.

629. Declarer should refuse the first trick, take the second spade, and lead a heart at once. After winning or establishing one heart trick, declarer can take the diamond finesse. By the time South wins the diamond finesse, he will be unable to return a spade unless the suit was originally 4-4. If declarer begins with the diamond finesse, the spades will be established, and North will get the lead with the ace of hearts in time to defeat the contract.

630. Declarer must refuse the first spade trick. The club finesse will eventually be taken towards the South hand, and West must guard against five spades to the ace-ten in the North hand with the king of clubs in the South hand.

631. Declarer should play low hearts from both hands. Nothing can be done if North has five hearts to the ace, with the king of diamonds in the South hand. If North has a six-card heart suit, however, the hold-up will save the contract.

632. Dummy must play low at the first trick. If hearts are continued, declarer takes the ace of clubs and ruffs his last heart. If hearts are abandoned, declarer can draw trumps and establish a diamond trick, with the ace of hearts as entry. It does declarer no good to take the first heart and return a heart, for then the defenders will lead a trump.

633. Declarer takes the ace of hearts and the ace of spades, cashes both top clubs, and ruffs a club with a high trump. If clubs break 4-2, dummy is entered with the nine of spades and another club is ruffed. Dummy is then re-entered with the king of spades and the established club can be cashed.

634. Declarer refuses the first trick but takes the second heart with the ace. He cashes both top clubs, discarding a diamond, and ruffs a club. He next takes the ace and king of spades and ruffs another club. Then he ruffs his remaining heart in dummy and cashes the last club, discarding a diamond.

635. Declarer takes the first heart, cashes the ace of diamonds, and ruffs a diamond. He gets to dummy with the nine of

spades to ruff another diamond and gets to dummy again with the ace of spades to ruff still another diamond. By this time, the king of diamonds should have dropped. Declarer gives up a heart trick, wins the club return with the ace, and ruffs a heart in dummy in order to get a discard on the queen of diamonds.

636. Declarer takes the ace of diamonds, the ace of clubs, and the ace of spades. He next ruffs a club in dummy and returns to his hand with a trump to the king. One more club ruffed in dummy should establish the suit and assure the contract.

637. West wins with the ace of hearts, takes both black aces, and draws one more trump if necessary. He next cashes the top diamonds, gets to dummy with a trump, discards a diamond on the extra high club, and ruffs a diamond. If the diamonds break 3-2, dummy can be re-entered with a trump for a final discard on a good diamond. If the trumps break 1-1, declarer can get to dummy three times with trumps and can thus guard against a 4-1 diamond break.

638. West wins with the ace of diamonds, takes the ace of spades, shifts to the ace of hearts, and ruffs a heart with a high trump. He enters dummy with the queen of spades to ruff another heart, draws trumps with the king of spades, and gets to dummy with diamonds to take his good cards in the red suits. If the jack of hearts becomes established, declarer has enough cards to assure the slam. Otherwise, he must try to develop a club trick.

639. Declarer wins with the ace of hearts, leads a trump to the queen and draws one or two more rounds of trumps, as needed, ending in his own hand. He then leads a heart towards dummy's jack. If North takes the queen of hearts and returns a club, dummy wins with the ace, and declarer discards the losing club on the jack of hearts. The queen of clubs is then led for a ruffing finesse. If South puts up the king, West ruffs. Otherwise, West discards a diamond. If North is able to win with the king of clubs, he cannot prevent West from getting to dummy with a trump in order to get two more discards on good clubs.

640. West wins with the queen of hearts and must develop the clubs in such a way as to keep South out of the lead. He therefore takes the second trick in dummy with the queen of clubs and returns a club towards his hand. If South plays low, West finesses the nine. Declarer should easily develop four clubs, assuring the contract. If the clubs are played carelessly, South may gain the lead and return a heart, allowing North to defeat the contract.

641. Declarer wins the diamond in either hand, takes the ace of spades, and finesses the next round of spades to make sure that South is kept out. If the finesse succeeds, declarer can draw trumps and run the diamonds. Even if the finesse loses, declarer can regain the lead and safely discard a heart on one of dummy's diamonds. If declarer fails to take the spade finesse, South may ruff the second or third diamond and lead hearts, giving North three heart tricks to defeat the contract.

642. Dummy wins with the king of hearts, and declarer must take the spade finesse at once. If the finesse loses, North cannot safely continue the attack on hearts. Declarer thus has time to develop his club tricks and to make his contract. If declarer goes after the clubs at the second trick, South may win and return a heart to establish North's suit. North may then regain the lead with the king of spades to defeat the contract.

643. Dummy should refuse the first trick! The plan is to discard a club on the ace of hearts, draw two rounds of trumps, cash the top clubs, and ruff a club. Dummy can be re-entered with a trump, and declarer discards two diamonds on the established clubs. If dummy wins the first trick, South may gain the lead with the third club and return a diamond through the king.

644. Dummy wins with the king of hearts and returns the king of clubs. If South plays low, West discards a heart. West does not mind giving up a trick to the ace of clubs since he can later draw trumps and discard two diamonds on the good clubs.

645. Dummy discards a club, and South is allowed to win

the first trick with the ace of spades. If a club is returned, West puts up the ace and draws trumps. He can discard dummy's remaining club on the king of spades, thus assuring the slam.

646. West should discard the seven of diamonds on the third round of hearts. This trick must be lost in any case. If South continues with a fourth heart, West should ruff with a low trump, ready to overruff in dummy if necessary. Nothing can be done if North has all of the missing trumps, but the contract is safe against any other distribution. If West makes the mistake of ruffing the third heart, North may overruff, and West will still have to lose a diamond.

647. Dummy discards a diamond on the third round of clubs! If clubs are continued, West can ruff and draw trumps. He will eventually ruff his third diamond in dummy. If dummy ruffs the third club, South may overruff. Declarer will still have to lose a diamond.

648. West wins with the king of diamonds, draws two rounds of trumps, cashes the ace of diamonds, and overtakes the heart in dummy to discard his last diamond on the other top heart. He then ruffs a diamond. If diamonds break 3-3, declarer gets back to dummy to discard on the last diamond. If North has four or more diamonds, the last diamond is led, and West discards a club (loser-on-loser), allowing North to win the trick. North must now return a club or give declarer a ruff and a discard. If the early play shows that *South* has the length in diamonds, declarer must eventually fall back upon the club finesse.

649. Declarer ruffs the second heart, takes the ace of spades, and enters dummy with the queen of diamonds to lead another spade. If South plays low, West finesses the nine or ten. This finesse may lose, but then the trumps will break 3-2. This safety play guards against four trumps in the South hand. If North has four trumps to both missing honors, nothing can be done.

650. Declarer wins the diamond in dummy, takes the ace of

hearts, and enters dummy with a diamond to lead the heart toward his hand. If South plays low, West finesses the ten. This is the same safety play as in No. 649. If South shows out on the second round of hearts, declarer must put up the ace and play for four spade tricks.

651. Declarer's only problem is to avoid the loss of two trump tricks. He should begin the trumps by leading the three to the ace. If both opponents follow, no more than one trick can be lost. If South shows out, a finesse can be taken through North. If North shows out, declarer can lead a trump to the king and another trump toward the jack.

652. Declarer wins with the king of diamonds and begins the trumps by taking the ace of clubs. There is no problem unless all four trumps are in one hand. If South has them all, nothing can be done. If North has them all, two finesses can be taken through him.

653. Dummy wins the first heart and immediately leads the jack of spades. There is no problem unless all the trumps are together. If North has them all, nothing can be done. If South has them all, two finesses can be taken through the 10-9.

654. West takes the king of hearts and leads a low club toward dummy. There is no problem unless one opponent holds all of the missing clubs. If North has them all and plays low, declarer can get back to his hand with the ace of clubs to lead another club towards dummy. If South has them all and wins the first trick, declarer can get back to dummy with the queen of clubs to finesse the A-9, and can return to dummy with a diamond to cash the last club.

655. Declarer wins with the king of spades, leads a diamond to the ace, and returns a diamond toward his hand. The idea is to guard against Q-10-x-x. If South plays low, West finesses the nine. If the finesse wins, all is well. If it loses, the suit will break 3-2. If South shows out on the second round of diamonds, West puts up the king and returns a diamond toward dummy's jack.

656. Declarer's problem is to restrict the trump loss to no more than two tricks. The best plan is to take the ace of hearts on the first round of that suit. If nothing startling happens, declarer gets to dummy with a spade or a club and returns a heart towards his queen. This guards against a singleton king of hearts in the North hand.

657. West must develop the clubs without losing more than one club trick. After drawing trumps, West should cash the ace of clubs. If no high cards drop, declarer can enter dummy and lead a club towards the queen. It would be fatal for South to finesse the queen of clubs and lose to a singleton king.

658. Dummy wins with the ace of diamonds, and declarer immediately tries the club finesse. If it loses, South must take the ace of spades in the hope of dropping a singleton king. If the club finesse succeeds, declarer can afford to lose one trump trick. For this purpose he should enter dummy and lead a low trump toward his hand. If South plays low, West should finesse the ten.

659. Declarer ruffs the first trick and begins the trumps by leading the ace. If North has them all, a finesse will hold him to one trump trick. If North shows out on the first round of trumps, the jack of hearts can be finessed around to South, and West is still in position to trump a spade, draw a trump with the ten, and enter dummy with a club to draw the last trump. If West incautiously leads a low trump to the king at the second trick, North may show up with all of the missing trumps and will defeat the contract by continuing spades.

660. West ruffs the second diamond and leads a low trump. If diamonds are continued, West ruffs again and leads the ace of trumps. With trumps breaking 3-2, West can now cash his good hearts and clubs, allowing an opponent to ruff whenever he pleases.

661. Dummy wins with the ace of diamonds, and declarer takes two rounds of trumps with the ace and king. He then knocks out the ace of clubs. If diamonds are continued, declarer

ruffs and continues to cash high clubs and hearts. West can afford to give up two trump tricks.

If declarer takes an early trump finesse, he will be forced to ruff a diamond. If trumps then break 4-2, one opponent will have as many trumps as declarer, with the ace of clubs still out. The defenders will have the chance to win with the ace of clubs and lead another diamond, thus causing West to lose control of the hand.

662. Dummy ruffs the first trick and declarer should immediately finesse the ten of hearts. Whether the finesse wins or loses, declarer should be able to control the spades and draw the trumps, after which the long clubs should provide all the tricks he needs. If declarer tries to draw trumps without a finesse, the loss of a *late* trump trick will allow the defenders to take two diamonds and two spades in addition to the trump.